Contemporary
sociology of
the school
General editor
JOHN EGGLESTON

The socialization
of teachers

CONTEMPORARY SOCIOLOGY
OF THE SCHOOL

COLIN LACEY

The socialization of teachers

METHUEN

First published in 1977 by Methuen and Co Ltd
11 New Fetter Lane, London ED4P 4EE
© 1977 Colin Lacey
Printed in Great Britain by
Richard Clay (The Chaucer Press), Ltd
Bungay, Suffolk

ISBN (hardbound) 0 416 56230 2
ISBN (paperback) 0 416 56240X

CONTENTS

Acknowledgements

This book has its origins in a research project into teacher socialization undertaken by a small team of social scientists between 1969 and 1973 and financed by the Social Science Research Council; the Tutorial Schools Research Project. I owe a considerable debt to the other members of that team, Mary Horton and Peter Hoad on whom I tried out many of the ideas developed in this book. I am indebted to the many people acknowledged within the final report of the project. I wish to underline here that without the collaboration and co-operation of the five education departments, their graduate student teachers and many practising teachers the research and therefore this book could not have been completed. It is my hope that in return this book will play a small part in deepening our understanding of the process of becoming a teacher and in strengthening the profession.

I owe a debt to Desmond Ryan for reading a number of the chapters in draft and to Jeanne Lacey for help with the preparation of the final draft. Morag Stalker and Pam Lloyd typed the final draft and assisted me in many ways.

Finally, the publishers and I would like to thank S. Winchester for permission to reproduce his article 'Another victim in the Ardoyne' from the *Guardian*, 30 October 1971, and C. Miller and M. Parlett and the Society for Research into Higher Education for permission to reproduce extracts from *Up to the Mark*.

Editor's introduction

Sociology has changed dramatically in the past decade. Sociologists have provided an ever increasing diversity of empirical and theoretical approaches that are advancing our understanding of the complexities of societies and their educational arrangements. It is now possible to see the over-simplification of the earlier sociological view of the world running smoothly with agreed norms of behaviour, with institutions and individuals performing functions that maintained society and where even conflict was restricted to 'agreed' areas. This normative view of society with its functionalist and conflict theories has now been augmented by a range of interpretative approaches in which the realities of human interaction have been explored by phenomenologists, ethnomethodologists and other reflexive theorists. Together they have emphasized the part that individual perceptions play in determining social reality and have challenged many of the characteristics of society that earlier the sociologists had assumed to be 'given'.

The new approaches have had striking effects upon the sociology of the school. Earlier work was characterized by a range of incompletely examined assumptions about such matters as ability, opportunity and social class. Sociologists asked how working-class children could achieve in the schools like middle class children. Now they also ask how a social system defines class, opportunities and achievement. Such concepts and many others such as subjects, the curriculum and even schools themselves are seen to be products of the social system in which they exist. In this study of the school we can see with special clarity the ways in which individual teachers' and students' definitions of the situation help to determine its social arrangements; how perceptions of achievement can not only define achievement but also identify those who achieve; how expectations about schooling can determine the nature and evaluation of schools.

This series of volumes explores the main areas of the sociology of the school in which new understanding of events is now available. Each introduces the reader to the new interpretations, juxtaposes them against the longer standing perspectives and re-appraises the contemporary practice of education and its consequences.

In each, specialist authors develop their own analyses of central issues such as poverty, opportunity, comprehensive schooling, the language and interaction of the classroom, the teacher's role, the ecology of education, and ways in which education acts as an instrument of social control. The broad spectrums of themes and treatments is closely interrelated; it is offered to all who seek new illumination on the practice of education and to those who wish to know how contemporary sociological theory can be applied to educational issues.

One important aid to understanding what happens in schools is the study of the behaviour of teachers. What are their views of the social system, their expectations for the different children they teach, their perceptions of the consequences of their teaching? Such orientations powerfully influence the kind of schooling available to all children. Although they are influenced by the nature of the school in which they work, teachers are also influenced by a series of other formative experiences – in particular their own education and their professional training. In *The socialization of teachers*, Colin Lacey examines the ways in which teachers think and act and the reasons that lead them to do so. Using previously unpublished research evidence he offers a set of new and highly important explanations to our exploration of the contemporary sociology of the school.

John Eggleston

Preface and overview

In the fall of the year several thousand college seniors get out of the casual college clothing, put on the uniform of the young executive – dark suit with a line of white handkerchief at the decreed distance parallel above the breast pocket – and present themselves to be interviewed ... (by the admissions committees of medical schools)

Howard S. Becker,
Boys in White (1961)

This is the first stage of what Becker himself calls 'one of the most compelling instances of personal change and development in adult life in our society'. The transformation of the social person, the persona, can be sudden. On the other hand, the inner or protected self is less subject to abrupt change and retains the ability to project itself through a variety of personae into a range of social situations. At the same time, even the deepest regions of the protected self are affected by the performances of the persona. These changes can be extensive, even if they are gradual.

This book examines the changes in the social person as students become teachers, but it also attempts to relate these changes to individual purposes and creativity. In keeping with

9

Gluckman's doctrine of naivety (1964) I do not attempt an investigation into the concept of self even though the present study has important implications for such an enquiry. Instead the book remains focused on the process of individual change in the context of changing institutional settings.

We know remarkably little about either process and this book reflects that deficiency. On the other hand, the book attempts to get beyond the narrowly utilitarian or doctrinaire study that has often characterized this field of enquiry and puts forward a way of looking at socialization that will help to broaden future studies.

I have not attempted a broad review of published work on teacher socialization, although a bibliography relevant to this task is included. The model of socialization emerges through an examination of a specific study of teacher training in which I took part between 1969 and 1973. The book recreates the process of the researcher learning about teacher socialization by getting close to data and the research process. It is not, however, a documentary on the research and the aim of presenting a view of teacher socialization remains dominant.

Chapter 1 seeks to establish the methodological and theoretical framework in which the study is presented. A brief critical examination of functionalist and conflict theories of socialization is undertaken. In line with a speculative essay by Dennis Wrong (1961), socialization is presented as a more complex, partial and incomplete, process than is normal in functional theory. It is suggested that the creative element in man's nature is responsible for a 'lack of fit' in the socialization process that is basic to an understanding of social change and should be studied by sociologists. This new orientation in sociology which includes the probing of the creative possibilities within social situations is described as the 'sociology of the possible' and distinguished from prescriptive or normative sociology.

Chapter 2 provides a context for the more detailed discussion of the socialization of teachers. Teaching is examined as a profession and a career and it is suggested that it is a divided profession giving rise to a number of careers. The role of the teacher is briefly examined in the context of rapid change in the structure of schools and the curriculum. Many of the changes affecting schools are similar in scale and direction to those affecting the colleges and universities in which teachers are trained. It is pointed out that these changes will affect the balance between constraining institutional forces and creative, innovating individuals. The case study of teacher socialization is introduced.

Chapter 3 introduces some of the major parameters affecting student-teacher socialization. The participant observation approach enables a 'grounded theory' development and the construction of a conceptual framework including subject subcultures, situationally constrained strategies and a modification of Becker's use of perspective. The aim is to reduce the emphasis on social or situational determinism that pervades earlier models of socialization.

Chapter 4 is a chronological description of the process of becoming a teacher. It traces the development of groups within a PGCE course through 'the honeymoon period' and 'crisis' until they 'learn to get by'. The description draws on the previously presented theoretical framework to deepen the understanding of this process – the adoption or creation of appropriate social strategies.

Chapter 5 takes the study beyond the confines of a single university PGCE course and introduces comparative data from five universities. This data is appropriate for studying broad patterns and movements in student opinion as they approach the full professional role. The interpretation of this data is informed by the previous analysis of the small scale study.

Chapter 6 examines the career. This is a much neglected area of study and the approaches adopted here are consequently limited. The first year of the career is illuminated by the open-ended responses of many of the teachers who qualified from the Sussex PGCE. The analysis enables some of the concerns of earlier chapters to be followed up within this data. The later career is examined through the re-analysis of a case study first presented in *Hightown Grammar* (1970). The limitations of the original analysis are exposed using the lessons learned from the present study. The analysis points to the need for a study of professional socialization which relates socialization and professional and institutional changes in a single framework.

Chapter 1

Sociologists are frequently accused of using complicated jargon where short everyday words will do. Why use 'teacher socialization' when 'learning to teach' is straightforward and avoids the problem of using a verb as a noun. 'Learning to teach' is easily understood and better English, so why not use it and avoid jargon? It would be easy to answer that one man's jargon is another man's terminology, and if people wish to learn sociology they must learn the terminology, just as students who learn medicine, astronomy or physics have to learn a great deal of complex and often unnecessary terminology. However, I find this line of argument particularly unattractive. It is important that new terms are introduced only if they have a job to do, for example, if they describe a new phenomenon or are more inclusive or exclusive than words already in use.

'Learning to teach' is certainly part of the process of teacher socialization, but it is only part of that process. Robert Merton (1957) has defined socialization as being:

> ... the process by which people selectively acquire the values and attitudes, the interests, skills and knowledge – in short the culture – current in groups to which they are, or seek to become, a member.

13

'Learning to teach' therefore corresponds to part of the definition – to acquiring the 'skills and knowledge'. The interests, values and attitudes of teachers are also of crucial importance in understanding the process of becoming a teacher, and much of the present book will be concerned with them. Something will also be said about the *selective* acquisition of values and attitudes, not only in the sense that selective acquisition differentiates teachers from non-teachers but also the way the profession is internally differentiated.

There are two more aspects of teacher socialization that are important to our discussion but are not developed in Merton's definition. Teaching is an occupation. The skills and values acquired are relevant to the teaching situation or situations where the individual is specifically identified as a teacher. They do not necessarily carry over into other situations. For example, some young teachers whose life-style is not conventionally associated with that of teachers may avoid stressful situations by insulating their in-school and out-of-school lives. So that, while it is important to recognize the power and pervasiveness of the occupation in generating values and attitudes, we should also be aware of the increasing freedom of the individual in a complex society to insulate one sphere of his/her life from another.

The second point represents a criticism of and an addition to Merton's definition. Merton talks of 'selectively acquiring values and attitudes' as though the values and attitudes were necessarily new to the individual concerned – a filling of empty vessels notion of socialization. It might well be that most of the values and attitudes are known to the teachers well before they become teachers; known to them when they were pupils, for example. What has changed is their own relationship to the classroom situation, that is their perspective. Teacher socialization therefore includes the process of developing a teacher perspective in which situations are both seen and interpreted in a new way.

To become a teacher is to become creatively involved with tasks and situations common only to teachers. It also involves being concerned with particular constraints, constraints that others do not have to subject themselves to. No other profession or occupation experiences exactly similar ones. These shared experiences and common problems give rise to a common set of interests, to certain ways of looking at the world, of interpreting the world and obtaining a world view – in short, a teacher perspective.

The importance of interpretation from a particular perspective is illustrated in the following examples – one a childhood memory, the second a contemporary reported incident from Northern Ireland. In each case the same incident is viewed from different perspectives and results in conflicting interpretations of the situation.

As a child of six or seven I witnessed an event that lodged in my memory. Two boys on a single bicycle swooped down a steep hill in a residential area of London. The wind streamed through their hair, their faces were tense with joy and excitement as they whooped and screamed down the steep concrete road. I can recall the whine and hum of the bicycle as it sped past. My childhood perspective interpreted the event as follows:

'two boys having fun, fantastic, wish I had a bicycle.'

The subsequent conversation between my mother and another housewife revealed a different interpretation:

'two boys doing something dangerous, glad it's not my son.'

If we include two hypothetical interpretations from other perspectives – the local policeman 'two boys breaking the traffic regulations'; and the local head-mistress 'two boys doing something irresponsible, bringing the school into disrepute' – we can appreciate the importance of perspective in applying appropriate and different values and judgements to a single event.

The second example is starker and more polarized. (It illustrates that perspectives are important in 'life and death' situations as well as trivial ones.) The paragraphs are extracted from an excellent report published by the *Guardian* in 1971. The paragraphs are grouped in columns to illustrate the contrasting interpretations of a single event: a man being shot.

Michael McLarnon was mending his Lambretta in the back of his home in the Ardoyne late on Thursday when he heard a commotion outside in the street and ran out to have a look. It was as he did so that Michael, a former British paratrooper and 'a peace-loving, God-fearing boy of 22' was hit by one of three shots

McLarnon was 'a known trouble-maker', and his home in Etna Drive was 'one of those we all come to memorise in time'.

McLarnon was standing at a street corner near his home, 'organising' a group of three other gunmen and a woman, who may or may not have been armed.

'He was waving a small revolver

fired by a British soldier.

'Those British bastards mowed him down without a word of warning. It was coldblooded murder,' his sister Mary said. 'He never did a thing wrong.'

'Michael was working in the back shed on his motorbike. He had been there all evening after he came back from work. He had worked in a paper-bag factory in Logniel ever since he had finished three months with the paratroops in Aldershot. And he hadn't missed a single hour since he joined.'

'We heard the binlids going at the front and Michael ran in from the back and out of the front door to have a look. His mother was a bit surprised because she had put his tea and chips out in the kitchen and he ran straight past them.

'He got out to the front and there were three shots. He fell back into the parlour, crying: "Mummy, I'm shot, I'm shot."'

His jacket had a gaping hole in the middle of the back and his blue Wrangler jeans were soaked in blackish blood from belt to turn-up. Four men, according to the family's alleged statement to an army inquiry team which arrived later, then took the body away.

There was no bullet hole to be seen in the brickwork near where his family said Michael had been shot – over a large bloodstain three feet from their front door step. 'But he was there and he didn't have a gun. He has never had one, and to prove it there'll be no IRA funeral for our Michael.'

'He was a God-fearing boy and he'll be given a good quiet

in the air, directing people in his group where to station themselves. Our marksman, who saw him clearly through his night-sight, asked the platoon commander for permission to fire at him. He was given the OK, fired a single round . . .'

According to the Green Howards their 10-man foot patrol was fired at from an alleyway at the rear of a group of houses in Etna Drive at 9.41 p.m. 'This time was logged against the word "contact",' an officer said. 'We had known something was going to happen. For three days it had been building up to a climax and when yesterday's ambush took place we were fully expecting it.'

Three shots were fired at the soldiers from the alleyway and then the sniper ran off, supposedly through one of the houses in Etna Drive. 'In a policy of hot pursuit, we had a perfect right to enter anyone's house to get at a gunman,' the Green Howards' spokesman said. 'Half the platoon got into the back door of a house and stationed themselves in the front room looking for the gunman out of the window. After a couple of minutes our marksman saw four men and a woman on a street corner about 25 yards away.'

Christian burial. But we might,'
his sister said, 'see funeral notices
from the local IRA units in
tomorrow's "Irish News". They
always put in a message of
condolence when an Irishman is
killed by these murderers. But it
won't mean that he was in the
IRA. He definitely wasn't.'

The accounts refer to a single event and yet there is hardly any
agreement about what happened – a provoked attack, an un-
provoked attack; about who was killed a known troublemaker
or a God-fearing boy; about how and where it happened – three
shots and on his own doorstep or one shot as he directed an
attack in the street. Learning to interpret what is seen or heard
is a central process in socialization. Central to this process of
learning to interpret is acquiring a perspective. It is quite possible that Michael McLarnon's values and attitudes as paratrooper
were very similar to those he took to his death. What changed as
he became an IRA gunman (if he ever did) was his way of selecting appropriate values for specific situations.

The discussion of socialization will be taken up throughout
the chapters of this book. The aim will be to obtain a picture or
model of the process, through the study of teachers, that is of
general relevance to understanding socialization. Before proceeding with this aim it is important to locate the study within the
alternative (complementary) models of society with which sociologists have worked since the beginning of their discipline – the
functionalist and conflict models.

Most sociology starts from a view of society. Indeed I would
argue that for a sociologist one of the essential reasons for undertaking a study of any aspect of society, no matter how trivial or
small scale, should be to clarify and build upon the view of the
wider society that he holds. Indeed if he fails to do this he fails
to undertake the central task of sociology. The short sketches of a
functionalist view of socialization and a conflict theorist's view
that follow are competing ways of looking at society that are
also to some extent complementary. In my view the tension that
exists in modern sociology between these theoretical models is one
of emphasis rather than exclusion and replacement.

Ways of looking at socialization

Functionalist model of socialization

The functionalist model stresses the notion that socialization fits the individual to society. One of the functions of the family, the school and the university is to do just that – to turn the 'barbarian invasion' of unsocialized infants, through a series of stages, into finished products capable of fitting into the various highly differentiated niches characteristic of modern industrial society. One of the features of functionalist models of socialization is therefore that they often envisage a process with an end, a finite product – a person fully matured and capable of taking his or her place in society. The number of stages in this process and the point in the development when it is deemed complete may vary from functionalist analyst to functionalist analyst, but the idea of a critical period of formation of basic personality structure followed by a series of stages building upon each other and progressively fitting the individual for a niche in society is common. It is true that functionalists sometimes talk of the mechanism of socialization proceeding throughout life, and of disfunctions and imperfect socialization, but this is usually no more than a slight deflection from their main task of establishing that the essential formative process of socialization occurs during childhood, and that basic patterns laid down during this period are built upon as the child becomes adolescent and adult. Some go further and argue that this is in fact essential to the stability and continued existence of society.

A second feature of functionalist accounts of socialization, derived from the basic notion of fitting the new individual to an already functioning society, is a characteristic view of the nature of man. Man is often portrayed as a relatively passive entity always giving way to socializing forces; an empty vessel to be filled with the basic value orientations and customs of the society of which he will become a part. In some cases he is seen in his infant stage as threatening, as savage and untutored to be tamed and formed by the groups to which he aspires. This emphasis is implicit in Merton's definition that I quoted earlier and is contained in Talcot Parsons' description of the socialization of the young (1951).

What has sometimes been called the 'barbarian invasion' of the stream of new-born infants is, of course, a critical feature of the situation in any society. Along with the lack of biological maturity, the conspicuous fact about the child is that he has yet to learn the patterns of behaviour expected of persons in his status in his society.

There is clearly a high degree of determinism in this view of society and the individual's relationship to it. The individual does not have much choice, he either joins or does not join the group in question. If he joins them he has to accept the norms and values of the group, for society or the group within society was there first and will be there after he has left. There is an appealing simplicity and obviousness about the whole structure of ideas so that it seems impossible to challenge it.

Many of these ideas were developed and taken up within sociology and social anthropology through the work of Emil Durkheim, who had published most of his major work by the end of the last century. They were developed in this country by social anthropologists, and indeed the ideas seemed to have particular relevance to unchanging societies with simple technology. For example, Radcliffe Brown wrote (1952):

Thus if I visit a relatively stable community and revisit it after an interval of ten years, I shall find that many of its members have died and others have been born; the members who still survive are now ten years older and their relations to one another may have changed in many ways. Yet I may find that the relations that I can observe are very little different from those observed ten years before. The structural form has changed little.

It is the emphasis on the structural form and the unchanging nature of social institutions that gives functionalism its deterministic character. For if a theoretical approach emphasizes the unchanging nature of institutions it must also give emphasis to the importance of the process by which succeeding generations of individuals fit into those institutions, that is socialization.

The conflict model of society and socialization

Functionalism as an approach to society has been criticized over the years by sociologists who espouse different approaches, each with its particular strengths and weaknesses. Conflict theorists have been quick to point out that functionalists were unable to explain the rapid changes that enveloped the emerging African states, even though functionalist anthropologists had spent much time and energy in describing traditional African societies (Rex, 1961). Conflict theorists argue that the cohesion of modern societies depends less upon the existence of highly complex and integrated value systems to which people subscribe than upon the domination of the majority by a minority. The power of the minority rests on its control of the system of production in any society, which in western society is industry. The agreement and cohesion to which functionalists point is therefore illusory and the power that cements modern industrial society is the economic power of the capitalist and managerial classes. The values and interests of the different classes are in fact in conflict but the dominant class is always striving to produce the illusion of cohesion and agreement.

It is clear from this short description that the conflict theorist's view of socialization is likely to be different from the functionalist's view at important points. Conflict between groups and within groups is likely to make socialization less straightforward in many ways. For example, if groups within society differ widely in their values and views of society then their children will tend to acquire values that differ from those of the people they meet when they leave the protection of the house and neighbourhood. This sort of conflict is of course most marked when, say, the children from working class homes go to schools where teachers and middle class pupils dominate the school. Class is not the only basis for this conflict; ethnic, political and religious differences can produce similar conflict.

Sociologists differentiate between primary and secondary socialization (see for example Berger and Luckmann, 1966). Primary socialization is socialization within the family. Secondary socialization is the process of induction into groups outside the family. Differences within secondary groups occur as soon as secondary groups are recruited from primary groups which are in themselves very different in culture. For example, the class-room composition of a comprehensive school is more likely to be mixed in its social class, ethnic or religious composition than, say, a grammar or secondary modern school within the old tri-partite system. It will also therefore contain less agreement about the purpose, style and importance of the activities within the classroom. Occupational groups will likewise exhibit differences as they recruit more widely across religious, ethnic, political and class boundaries. These within-group differences give rise to stresses within the socialization process. Socialization becomes a strategically important area and an arena for conflict and competition.

We can expect conflict theorists to look for differences within and between groups; to stress the fact that the individual will be confronted with choices that represent a wide spectrum of variation at any point in the socialization process. On the other hand, functionalists will stress that differences can have reciprocal and integrating functions. They are concerned with the central tendency in groups that they study, and differences from this central tendency are often neglected or regarded as damaging and deviant. The following quotation from Talcot Parsons (1951) illustrates the 'filling empty vessels syndrome' and his preoccupation with the central tendency.

Our present discussion is not concerned with the fact that children, having learned these patterns, tend very widely to deviate from them, though this, of course, happens at every stage, but with the process of acquisition itself on the part of those who have not previously possessed the patterns.

Quite clearly, both ways of looking at society are borne out by some aspects of society more than others, and to give prominence to one is not to destroy completely the value of the other. Nevertheless the account that follows is biased towards accepting the 'conflict' view of society as a basis for description and analysis. There are a number of reasons for this.

The assumptions and implications of conflict models of society fit with my own view of society, which is, of course, in turn derived from my experience within society – my biography.

Functionalist models are, on the admission of many functionalists, best suited to the exploration and understanding of relatively unchanging societies. But societies in all parts of the world are now in a process of rapidly accelerating change. Economic and technological change in methods of production is only one aspect of this change. The rate of technical change has enabled or forced massive social change, vast migrations of population, enormous increases in the complexity of life, in the scale of organizations, in the specialization of individuals and the division of labour and rapid change in the distribution of power. Individuals in industrial society no longer grow up and live in isolated specialized communities. They can no longer expect to start and complete their working life in the same speciality. In a relatively short career I have worked in a factory, on a farm, in a hospital, in schools and universities. I started my first degree as a geologist, started my M.A. in social anthropology, my Ph.D. in sociology and am now a professor of education. I have lived in four large industrial conurbations in two continents and now live in Brighton. Such changes may be unusual, but they are becoming the normal pattern for an increasingly large minority of people – including some teachers. They bring with them the need to develop new understandings about the process of socialization; about the relationship between the individual and a society in which new tensions and conflicts are constantly being created.

Finally, I feel it is important that this account should challenge many aspects of functionalist models of socialization because teachers and educators often see the world in common sense functional terms in which conflict and change are seen in a negative light. The alternative is presented in this book as a model of partial or incomplete socialization. Socialization is presented as a more complex, interactive, negotiated, provisional process. The model presented here also stresses the importance of man as a creative force, as a searcher for solutions and as possessing a considerable potential to shape the society in which he lives. This potential has in many cases yet to be realized by many who accept society as given.

Prescriptive, positivist and interpretative sociology

Authors who write about society have characteristically been classified along a continuum with analysis at one pole and prescription at the other. Prescriptive writers include many political, religious and educational reformers who write from a set of a priori assumptions, often hidden and unrealized, about the nature and state of society and/or man. Treatments are then prescribed either in terms of some action to be taken or some set of beliefs to be encouraged. Prescriptive writers clearly vary enormously in the quality of argument produced, and quality and quantity of the evidence produced, and the amount of prescription. In education they range from Sir C. Norwood (1943) to I. D. Illich (1971) and from A. S. Neill (1962) to Rhodes Boyson (1975). They do, however, share a purpose, they write about 'what ought to be'. It may or may not be in existence and it may or may not be possible. Sociologists have at times self-consciously adopted this stance; the work of Lester Ward (1924), who wrote of education as the 'means of progress' is a good example.

At the other end of the continuum the major concern is an analysis of 'what is'. There is a great deal of dispute about how and how far this can be achieved. The two schools of thought that we shall examine briefly are the positivist and the interpretative schools.

On the one hand positivist sociologists are concerned with establishing 'facts' about society (Durkheim called them social facts and recommended that social facts be treated as 'things'), which are objective indicators that tell the sociologist something about the state of society, rather like the temperature tells the doctor something about a patient. Durkheim attempted to establish a 'normal' rate of suicide for a given society and used the fluctuations in the rate to diagnose different 'conditions' of that society. It is clear that Durkheim brought a biological method of classification and measurement to the study of society. Other sociologists have been less extreme and less rigorous than Durkheim, but have still concentrated on measuring, for example, rates of crime or other recorded statistics. Others have used questionnaires to discover the 'objective' characteristics of the group being studied, say, the social class composition of the group. All kinds of models derived from other disciplines have been adapted for use in the study of society. Ecological models have been borrowed from biology, system and cybernetic models from mathematics, and comparative input-output models from demography. Sociologists using this type of 'hard' data and models adapted from the sciences have often been labelled positivists. Their approach has been challenged by interpretive sociologists who criticized the use of and reliance on statistical data. They argue that the attempt to imitate science and obtain 'objective' data is misguided and it distracts from the real tasks of sociology. The recording of a 'crime' is not the recording of an objectively classifiable event. It depends on an act being recognized as criminal by people who can successfully label it as criminal and who can persuade 'important others' to label it as criminal. If a catering manager takes a chicken home on the back seat of his car for his family's weekend dinner, it may be regarded as within his rights (his perks) by the people who are likely to notice or know about it. If the lady who does the washing up attempted to take the chicken home in her shopping bag, she might well be noticed, accused of stealing, and the accusation

23

would very likely be upheld. The complex set of understandings, the 'perks hierarchy', surrounding the management of the preparation and serving of food, would have been breached. Similarly, a headmaster who keeps a school tape recorder at home on indefinite loan is unlikely to be accused of theft.

The statistic is not an objective distillation of similar events. These events need to be interpreted and given meaning and in this process unpredictable and unstudied (by the positivist) variation takes place. The interpretive sociologist is centrally interested in this process. He ignores the statistic and looks deeply into the behaviours? Why is there a variation in this interpretive process? Why are some interpretations more potent than others? Why do these potent interpretations eventually define the situation for a whole group? There is also a wide variety of approaches within the interpretive school.

The analytical end of the continuum is not without its common problems. For both the positivist and the interpretive sociologist the values and purposes of the investigator enter into the study at the level of posing questions, observation and recording. The events that the interpretive sociologist chooses to record are not guaranteed as typical except through an appeal to the reader's own experience and the output of the sociological profession as a whole. But it must be remembered that the interpretive sociologist is less concerned with establishing generality and more concerned with the interpretation and understanding of social processes. The essence of both approaches is that there are agreed upon procedures for minimizing and/or understanding the ways in which the values of the investigator enter into the research and analysis. Each approach is in effect a different set of emphases and strictures in order to gain an analytical insight. It is my view that one of the emerging strengths of modern sociology is that it is now possible to choose from a wide range of approaches. As yet very few sociologists span the range satisfactorily and many of the variants are so new that their strengths and weaknesses are still partly unknown. Sociology is now poised at the beginning of an exciting new phase in which the potential of new approaches is being tested and evaluated. The following section of this chapter advocates one such new approach and points to its relevance in the study of socialization.

The sociology of the possible

We have distinguished prescriptive from analytical sociology. In practice the dividing line is often by no means clear cut. There have been a number of pleas from within the sociological profession for the establishment of two distinct and academically respectable disciplines for the study of education. Hansen (1967) has proposed the titles: the sociology of education for the analytical study of education and educational sociology for the prescriptive or normative study of education. As Hansen points out the dangers of not distinguishing these studies are obvious. Personal prejudice masquerading as analysis is one, and Hansen enumerates a number of others. It is unlikely, in my view, that these distinctions will take root. The prestige of the analytical approach is such that the study of education is unlikely to develop in the direction proposed by Hansen. Sociologists will continue to present their work as analytical even though it contains large prescriptive elements. It will require the critical appraisal of colleagues and others to locate and identify the prescriptive bias.

The major preoccupation of sociologists has been and will continue to be with the 'as it is now', that is with the analysis of the existing networks of social relationships. There is an important limitation to this mode of investigation. It fails to explore the degree to which a particular social organization is what it is, because of the lack of alternatives that are possible within the constraints of the situation. A given form of social organization could be the only possible form or it could be one of a number of possibilities. In other words, within the usual analytical approaches in sociology there is no measure or understanding of the flexibility in a given situation. We should note that the sociologist of the 'as it is now' is not being asked to become the sociologist of the 'ought to be', but the sociologist of the 'could be' or the possible. We shall see later that within the study of the 'possible' he is expected to retain an analytical approach.

The nearest that the sociologist has traditionally approached this study has been to look at the naturally existing variation in social organization. Let us look at an example of a traditional analytical approach and see where the sociology of the possible could develop. To discover the variation within a school organization the sociologist might conduct a survey and conclude that the variations in streaming or pastoral organization or age-grouping that he found, demonstrated the possible variation within the society he was studying. But this is just the mistake that functionalist anthropologists made in their studies of African communities in the pre-war and early post-war years. To avoid this, the sociologist could look carefully at the organizations concerned to discover where the growth points were. For example, in a study of school organization and streaming he/she might find initially that there was a near normal distribution of an index indicating the homogeneity of classrooms.

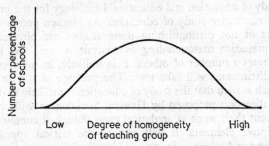

Figure 1.1 *Where homogeneity in high streaming is well developed*

When this curve is looked at in more detail, he/she might then discover that certain types of school present different distributions.

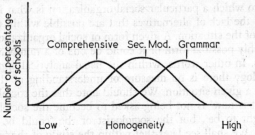

Figure 1.2

If the sociologist knows that comprehensive schools are increasing at the expense of grammar and secondary modern schools, he/she might conclude that mixed ability in teaching groups was increasing. Our hypothetical sociologist might increase the sophistication of the study by undertaking a number of case studies of the various types of school and the peculiar circumstances which constrain them.

The sociology of the possible continues beyond where the

26

normal sociological approach finishes. The sociologist becomes particularly interested in the study of innovation for example, schools where the staff are attempting to change the curriculum or organization for a particular educational purpose. The study of innovation as collective resocialization is at the heart of the concern of the sociologist of the possible. The limits of the possible may be illuminated by the study of failed innovations. Cases, where the staff have attempted to make significant changes but have been defeated by the problems they have encountered, like Tyndale and Risinghill are of importance, but so are less spectacular instances where innovations have been quietly lost in the normal day to day activities of the school. In order to perceive when and where aspects of the change meet opposition and are scaled down or dropped, the sociologist must become involved in working with those groups of teachers who wish to make significant change. The whole set of constraints which mould and form the innovation must be the concern of the sociologist of the possible as he centres on the relationship between individual and collective purpose and social structure. In some circumstances it may be necessary for the sociologist to become part of the creative process of change.

For example, in a study of an open plan school which planned to develop a collaborative teaching style involving the co-operative sharing of resources the researcher was able to document the process by which individual teachers gradually removed themselves and their resources from the scheme. The ideology of this innovation in co-operation remained intact while the main aspects of it were being, sometimes unwillingly and sometimes unknowingly but nevertheless persistently, dismantled. The strains that developed within the co-operative process and brought about the decay were not communicated within planning meetings and at no stage became a major concern of the head teacher. Once the major components of the analysis were clear, one strategy for the sociologist of the possible would be to devise a way of communicating his findings, through seminars and working parties. The aim of the working parties could be to find collective solutions to the problems exposed. At this stage in the research the sociologist comes closest to losing his analytical stance. In doing so he does not necessarily move away from the analytical end of the continuum presented above. If he/she becomes involved in the generation of change, for example by writing part of a curriculum, or helping to teach within the newly designed programme, he runs the risk of being drawn into the promotion and advocacy of a particular change and drawn out of the business of analysis into the business of prescription. But none of these activities are taboo, if they fit into the design of the research and do not prevent the researcher from regaining his prime purpose, which is his analytical stance. This form of intervention may be *necessary* to test the limits of the possible. This is because the resources brought by the researcher (analytical insight or simply more manpower) can be used legitimately to augment the resources of the innovating group and test the limits of the possible at a higher level of energy input. Although there are developed methodologies within sociology under the broad heading of participant observation that will enable him to cope with the strains inherent in this situation, the danger remains and in the end the professional judgment of his colleagues and others is an important corrective.

The relevance of the sociology of the possible to sociological theory on the one hand and to people within a particular institution or section of society on the other, is not difficult to establish. By examining institutions undergoing change or innovations within organizations the sociologist can begin to point to how far flexibility exists within a social structure. Beyond this his study of individuals changing their behaviour and developing new patterns of relationship should begin to establish new patterns and possibilities in the link between the individual and society which is an area of crucial importance to the theorist.

Individuals who are in the process of becoming part of an established organization are in a very different position from a group who are collectively changing their behaviour to fulfil an idea and who are hoping to proceed to an as yet non-existent form of social organization, for example, team teaching. The second group are involved in an effort of collective resocialization and the strains and uncertainties of this sort of activity are only slowly becoming clear to us. For the teacher involved in a curriculum or organizational innovation there are no existing models on which to mould oneself, no assurances of success if certain criteria are fulfilled and more importantly no certainty that others are putting their effort in the same direction and to the same effect. In the past and in other areas of society, ideological commitment and charismatic leadership have compensated for some of these uncertainties. In schools today there is a mistrust of the 'expert' and the charismatic prophet of change who brings simple blanket solutions for complex problems. There is a need for local, careful, analytical approaches to problems in which teachers participate closely with the researcher, each learning from the other.

The relevance of 'the possible' to the study of socialization is clear from the above. If socialization is an incomplete and partial process and the limits of a social situation depend at least to some extent on the creativity and skill of the participants, then the sociology of the possible becomes, on the one hand, a method of charting the flexibility of social structures and, on the other, a way of testing and refining our view of the process of socialization.

Chapter 2

Introduction

In this study, the process of socialization is viewed as the development of sets of behaviours and perspectives by an individual as he confronts social situations. Quite clearly these behaviours and perspectives change most quickly and dramatically if the social situations which confront the individual change rapidly. It is clear from Northern Ireland, the Lebanon and other places that individuals who have lived in peaceful proximity for years can quickly change and become members of rival militias bent on mutual destruction. In the normal run of things the changes faced by an individual or group are gradual. They are most *rapid* during changes of status, changes of job or changes produced by social disruption. Some of these phenomena are more difficult to study than others. Rapid changes of status that take place within an institutional setting, such as qualifying as a teacher, are much easier to study than diffuse and scattered changes that take place in a large number of institutions, for example becoming a head of department or a headmaster. It follows that studies of students and even probationary teachers are much more common than teachers in mid-career or nearing retirement. The account of teacher socialization as a career-long process will therefore be difficult to sustain. While there are hundreds of studies of teachers in training, I know of no study of teachers approaching retirement. It will be possible to compensate for this imbalance in the literature by stressing a theoretical approach that is appropriate to both situations (initiation and retirement), but it will inevitably lead to a considerable overall imbalance. The main emphasis will be on the early years of training and professional socialization.

In this chapter we will examine some of the major parameters of teaching under three headings: teaching as a career, teaching as a role, and teacher-training. This discussion will provide the context for the more detailed description of material in later chapters. It will be important to establish the rapidly changing pattern of preparation for teaching and the organization and context of teaching while at the same time realizing that many of the problems faced by teachers remain untouched. This is particularly so in the field of teacher education.

Teaching as a career

The idea of a career, a progress through life, incorporates some notions of continuous process that are in keeping with our conceptual framework and in line with our major purpose.

Teaching is one of a number of careers loosely classified as a profession. Sociology – Jackson (1970), Leggatt (1970), Johnson (1972) – have spent a considerable amount of time trying to define what precisely is meant by the term profession and whether teaching qualifies or not. Etzioni (1969) puts teaching within the category of semi-profession in which he also groups social workers and nurses, that is, groups who work in complex organizations, often under the control of others. Johnson, on the other hand, is more concerned with the power that the profession exercises over conditions, organization and nature of work on a national level as well as a day to day basis. Others have put emphasis on the mysterious and protected nature of the knowledge the group possesses. Teachers are clearly marginal and unusual on a number of counts.

Teaching is traditionally a divided profession. It is divided by the expertise and understandings that the professionals bring to the classroom; it is divided by the status and function of the institutions in which they serve; it is divided by the training, professional and social origins of its members; and, of increasing importance, it is divided by the aims and purposes attached to that element they hold in common, their teaching (pedagogy). In addition, it is the only major profession that deals almost exclusively with children. The age specialization of teachers (infants, sixth form, etc.) provides another set of divisions that are not related to major areas of concern outside teaching, for example in research, or academic disciplines. Finally, it has a high proportion of women among its members.

Let us examine in more detail some of these structural divisions within the profession. It may well be that the divisions within the profession give rise to a number of rather than a single career pattern.

Teachers as a group are normally reported as predominantly women; 'slightly over two thirds of the profession are women ...' writes one inaccurate commentator. In fact, the proportion of women depends on how the category 'teacher' is defined. We can see from the 1973 figures that the proportion of men fluctuates between subdivisions. Generally men tend to be concentrated in schools teaching the older children or colleges teaching the more technical subjects.

Table 2.1

March 1973	Men	Women	Total
Primary (Maint.)	45,000	141,800	186,800
Secondary (Maint.)	110,200	82,600	192,800
Special	4,300	6,700	11,000
Direct Grant	4,100	3,900	8,000
Further education	49,800	9,400	58,200
Church education	7,500	3,500	11,000
	Total – 475,300		

Note: By January 1975, the number of full-time teachers in all forms of educational establishment other than universities exceeded 500,000. This was the culmination of a rapid and uninterrupted expansion of the profession since the 1944 Act. In 1946–47 teachers in maintained primary and secondary education numbered 177,000; by 1974–75 it had reached 420,000. This expansion has now been halted by the drop in numbers of children of school age and the 'cuts' in education.
Source: *Statistics in Education* HMSO (1973)

If we look in more detail at men and women teachers in primary and secondary schools, we can see that despite the large number of women, men predominate in the top jobs. Women are concentrated on the lowest rung of the ladder.

Table 2.2

	Men	Women	Women as % of men	Women Grads. as % of men Grads.
Maintained primary school teachers				
Head Teachers	13,521	10,128	74·9	26·1
Deputy heads	6,870	10,299	149·9	61·4
Scale 5	23	13	—	—
Scale 4	533	715	134·1	53·2
Scale 3	5,064	9,114	179·9	77·2
Scale 2	8,402	27,720	329·9	141·6
Scale 1	10,613	84,838	799·4	294·0
Secondary school teachers				
Head Teachers	4,295	1,050	24·4	18·7
Deputy Heads	3,964	2,230	56·3	41·6
Senior Teachers	865	167	19·3	17·3
Scale 5	9,638	2,261	23·5	23·3
Scale 4	25,313	9,584	37·9	34·3
Scale 3	19,708	12,088	61·1	59·4
Scale 2	18,267	16,104	88·2	88·7
Scale 1	27,434	37,544	136·8	108·9

Source: *Statistics in Education* HMSO (1973)

It is apparent that within teaching men and women continue to experience differing constraints and opportunities. We can use the salary structure to illustrate one aspect of this. Teachers are paid on three criteria – initial qualification, length of service and responsibility of the post held. If we construct a graph of salaries earned in each age group for men and women of similar qualifications (graduate, non-graduates) then the different heights of the graph will illustrate the differences in responsibility payments made.

It is quite clear from both graduate and non-graduate curves that men earn more than women and this difference starts to emerge early in the career. The differences are due to a career structure that favours men. Women may have to interrupt their career with childbirth and child rearing and diminish their opportunity to earn length of service payments. They may well have family responsibilities during their work that prevents them

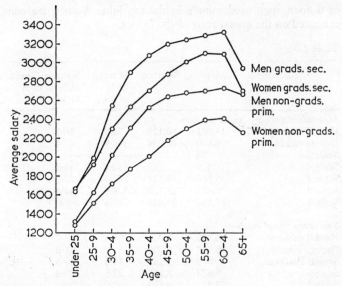

Figure 2.1 *Average salaries of full-time teachers against age (1973)*

taking on additional responsibilities. The 'wastage' rates indicate a higher 'wastage' for women, particularly between the ages of 20 and 39.

While it is clearly necessary for women to take periods away from teaching for childbirth, the *effect* of this absence on career is a matter of negotiation and agreement. This is surely one area where rapid change of traditionally accepted structures might occur in the near future.

The differences that emerge between men and women within teaching are paralleled by a set of factors that influence recruitment and the standing of teaching among other professions. It is clear that men and women differ in their career perspectives. Women grow up in a world where there are relatively few women doctors, lawyers, engineers and city financiers. Their choice of career is influenced by their early impressions of what is, and what is not, possible within this world view. Teaching stands out as a relatively well paid, secure job which is easily accessible. It compares well with nursing, social work and secretarial work, which are the other traditional occupations for qualified women.

There is a contrasting situation for men. The older, better paid professions are male preserves. The boys' public schools still provide direct and preferential access to them, and working-class boys often grow up in a world where these professions are hardly visible. The table below, from Floud and Scott's work on teacher recruitment, illustrates the effect of these factors on the social class composition of the teaching staffs of various types of school.

Table 2.3 *Social origins of teachers in grant earning schools, England and Wales, 1955*

Father's Occupation	Type of School							
	Primary		Modern		Maint. Gram.		D.G. Gram.	
	Men %	Women %	Men %	Women %	Men %	Women %	Men %	Women %
Professional and Administrative	6·0	8·8	7·5	11·4	12·5	17·8	19·8	30·4
Intermediate	48·3	52·2	45·9	54·8	55·1	63·1	61·5	57·4
Manual	45·7	38·9	46·7	33·8	32·4	19·1	18·6	12·2
	100·0	100·0	100·0	100·0	100·0	100·0	100·0	100·0

Source: Floud and Scott (1961)

The higher social class origins of women in the profession is clearly exhibited in all types of school. This phenomenon is borne out by the most recent studies of university departments and colleges of education. The table also illustrates a second of the divisions within the teaching profession which were described earlier. Each type of school differs in prestige and function within our stratified society. As a result, recruitment to each type of school shows marked differences in the social class origins of its teachers. The range is greatest in the percentage of men teachers from working-class families teaching in secondary modern schools (46·7 per cent) to those in direct grant grammar schools (18·6 per cent). The range would be greater if data for public schools were available. Becker (1953) has described the status differences of schools within the North American public school system as giving rise to a characteristic career pattern, moving from inner city to suburb. In England a corresponding pattern has been inhibited by the academic status difference between secondary modern schools and grammar schools, but as comprehensive schools emerge from the present reorganization a similar pattern is likely to develop.

The division produced by the status and function of schools has its counterpart in the training of teachers. Academic schools have traditionally been staffed by teachers drawn from the universities who qualify for teaching by taking a postgraduate certificate in education within a university or college department of education. Other schools have in the past been staffed mainly by college-trained teachers who take a more general professional qualification, a certificate, instead of a degree. In this respect teaching differs markedly from the older professions.

A number of changes have blurred the distinction – comprehensive schools have now replaced the tripartite division of schools in many parts of the country; colleges now offer B.Eds to a proportion of their intake, the majority of university graduates now take their PGCE within colleges of education, and the Open University has enabled many college-trained teachers to up-grade their qualification. The basic divisions still remain, as the table below illustrates.

Table 2.4 *Students admitted to courses of initial training*

PGCE	1970	1971	1972	1973
University Depts. of Education	4,962	5,032	5,134	4,828
Colleges of Education	2,388	3,987	5,124	5,297
Colleges of Education 4 year (B.Ed.) 3 year (Cert.)	34,044	35,188	34,859	32,468

Source: *Statistics in Education* HMSO (1973)

It is perhaps an inescapable conclusion that teaching represents a number of careers. Rather than a single strand there appear to be a number of strands leading to markedly different careers for the various categories of teacher that we have examined. In fact the variation is even greater than indicated here. Wastage rates from the profession are extremely high and research suggests that school teaching is sometimes used as a starting point for careers in a number of kindred occupations, for example, administration, research, publishing, journalism and social work.

It is almost inevitable that any statement about 'teachers' reflects more closely the state of affairs affecting one career strand than another. This book is based on a study of graduate teachers at five departments of education. It will be important to remember that this is the case and that statements made are not necessarily typical of all teachers' careers. There are, on the other hand, grounds for believing that as the profession moves towards an all-graduate profession, it will be moving towards the kind of professional structure described in this book. These changes are described later in this chapter.

A number of research monographs published over the last five years have pointed up deep divisions within the profession that result from basic philosophies about the purpose of education. The most substantial of these monographs describes the work done by Barker-Lunn (1970) into the effects of streaming in primary schools. She found that a research project that was initially looked upon as investigating an organizational arrangement turned out to be examining basic philosophies. Streaming, the organization of children in the school, was only a superficial indicator of this deeper phenomenon. Under the heading 'Streamed and non-streamed schools embody different philosophies' she wrote:

... schools using streaming or non-streaming did not merely differ in organization. The streamed school seemed to be more systematic in its approach, concentrated more on 'traditional' lessons, gave more emphasis to the 3Rs and was, at least overtly, more authoritarian. Its staff was likely to approve of bright children, of eleven-plus selection and of streaming as a means of adapting to individual differences. The non-streamed school presented an apparent contrast. Its teachers held more 'permissive' views on such things as cleanliness and manners, were more tolerant of noise and talking in the classroom, and disapproved of the differentiation implicit in streaming and the eleven-plus procedures. Their teaching tended to place more emphasis on self-expression, learning by discovery and practical experience. In short, the aims and practices of the two kinds of school seemed to embody different views about children and different philosophies of education.

Barker-Lunn went on to show that different types of teacher embodied these philosophies and were more likely to teach within schools that practised them. Incidentally her research showed no difference in academic performance, on a wide range of tests, resulted from these different streaming policies. Bennett (1976) found similar differences between teachers in his study of teaching styles in primary schools. He found a more complex picture of styles than Barker-Lunn but was still able to condense them into three categories along the traditional-progressive dimension described in the quotation. His findings relating to pupil progress, on a much smaller sample than the NFER study, run counter to the results that would be expected from an interpretation of Barker-Lunn's results.

The aims and purposes of education are central to the art of teaching and the process of socialization. The issue will be taken up again in later chapters. It is useful to note at this point that although other professions are not usually thought of as being rent with this sort of fundamental disagreement it is by no means as clear-cut as this. Medicine, law, social work, architecture and many others are all situated at points of potential fundamental controversy. Controversy of this sort has in fact arisen in some of them, for example architecture and social work, and more lately medicine. In the older professions it is probably the pattern of recruitment that has protected them for so long.

One aspect in which teaching is unmistakably professional is in the earning patterns of its members over their careers, although the method of remuneration is more bureaucratic (salary) than professional (fees). If the career structure is portrayed by the mean annual earnings, for each five year cohort, the resulting curve (see p. 39) displays the characteristic shape of many professional occupations. The curve mounts steeply as the teacher increases in experience (rewarded by yearly increments) and takes on early responsibilities (rewarded by responsibility allowances). The curve then flattens out to a gentle slope which indicates continuing small increases in responsibility (rewarded by enlarged responsibility allowances, yearly increments cease) until the age of sixty. A small decline in average earning power then takes place, probably due to ill health, early retirement, etc. If this curve is seen as depicting the way society rewards changes in the job being carried out (changes in the social situations being met by the individuals in each cohort) then it can be interpreted as, very roughly, depicting the rate of change in the socialization process. Quite clearly this can be very different for some sub-groups within the profession, for example, headmasters. If the graph is extended slightly and the student and retirement phases are included, the abrupt and spectacular changes at recruitment and retirement are also depicted. The resulting curve is depicted schematically and compared with that of manual workers, and the contrasting features become apparent.

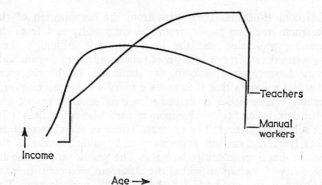

Income

Age ⟶

Note: The diagram does not accurately represent differentials

Source: *Statistics in Education* HMSO (1973)

Figure 2.2

The role

The role of the teacher has been written about extensively in sociology and education (Westwood, 1967, 1969; Wilson, 1962; Floud, 1962; Kob, 1961; Hoyle, 1969). The general exploratory writings of the early 1960s were followed by a number of empirically based writings in the late 1960s and early 1970s (Kelly, 1970; Musgrove and Taylor, 1969; Grace, 1972; Finlayson and Cohen, 1967). These investigations were predominantly questionnaire based and theoretically naive, but they added an interesting dimension to our understanding of teaching – the way teachers perceive their own role. More recently sociologists have turned their attention to the actual performance of the teacher's role within the classroom (Chanon and Delamont, 1975; Stubbs and Delamont, 1976; Delamont, 1976; Hamilton, 1975; Walker and Adelman, 1975; Walker, 1972). These writers have been centrally concerned with the study of the interaction of teacher and pupils within the classroom. They have often worked within symbolic interactionist or anthropological frameworks and have added a further dimension to our understanding of the teacher's role.

My interest in teacher socialization derives from my own experience of teaching in a comprehensive school and early research experience in a grammar school. These experiences left me in no doubt about the enormously powerful constraints of the classroom situation. They stem from the organization of the classroom and the pupils, from the community and from the teaching profession and the local authority. Although these pressures derive from a number of sources and vary considerably from classroom to classroom, the similarities of the classroom situation are such that it imposes a unity on the teaching profession. Waller (1932) described schools as 'unstable despotisms' – the description fits the classroom in particular better than it fits the school in general. The unstable nature of the classroom derives from the marked asymmetry and 'public' nature of the teacher–pupil relationships within it. The 'public' in this case are the thirty-plus children within the classroom who constitute the object and the audience for the teacher's performance. The dynamism and quicksilver fluidity of these relationships need to be experienced to be believed; a fact of life that beginning teachers learn very quickly. The despotism derives from the legal/historical convention that the teacher is responsible for the 'learning' and 'order' within the classroom. These dimensions influence the teacher's role more positively than any philosophy of education can hope to achieve by exhortation or persuasion. Hilsun and Cane (1971) have discovered that teachers spend only 46 per cent of their time teaching within the classroom, but this quantification tells us nothing about the over-riding importance of the classroom in shaping the role of the teacher. The recent concentration of research effort on the classroom is not misplaced.

The final characteristic of the classroom that has shaped the teacher's role and the culture of the school over the years has been its isolation. The isolation has been twofold. On the one hand there was separation of one teacher from another and on the other hand there was the separation from other members of the teacher's role-set – LEA officials, members of the community and, in particular, parents. The traditional organization of the school as a series of discrete classrooms, each with a lone teacher supported by an administrative structure geared to sustain him only in those matters directly related to academic 'learning' and 'order', has only recently changed. Even in the 1950s, the organizational structure of many schools consisted of the timetable, a system for supplying books, chalk and other essentials (the stock cupboard) and a set of rules and punishments concerning discipline. In small schools this support structure was provided entirely by the head and a part-time school secretary and in larger schools by the head, a senior master and a secretary. In the late 1950s more complex social organizations began to develop. For example, house systems in secondary schools and family groupings in primary schools were established that were aimed at providing a richer social environment. The growing awareness of the social context of education, fed by sociological analysis of the education system on the one hand and the perplexing problems of the classroom on the other, led to a broadening of the teacher's role and a more complex school organization. Wilson (1962) picked up this development in his *British Journal of Sociology* essay and stressed the growing diffuseness of the teacher's role as a cause of growing dissatisfaction. The empirical studies that followed stopped short of a thorough investigation of Wilson's analysis but were able to show that most teachers still had a very narrow perception of their role. Musgrove and Taylor (1969) found that teachers saw themselves as overwhelmingly concerned with 'instruction in subjects' and 'moral training', and only slightly concerned with 'social training', 'family life', 'social advancement' and 'citizenship'.

It is interesting to note that Musgrove and Taylor considered that they had contradicted Wilson's argument but in fact they largely missed the point. Wilson's analysis came close to an exercise in the sociology of the possible. He argued from *developments* that he saw growing within the teaching profession. Musgrove and Taylor answered with a one-shot survey of teachers' perceptions of their role, which is a totally inadequate method of countering an argument about emergent social change.

Musgrove and Taylor's survey went on to reveal an interesting discrepancy between teachers' perception of their own role and what they imagined to be the view of parents. Teachers saw parents as largely indifferent to 'moral training' but very concerned with 'social advancement'. In fact the survey revealed parents and teachers to be almost identical in their views. The researchers concluded that the massive discrepancy revealed by their study resulted from a lack of an effective means of communication between teachers and parents.

This conclusion supports the argument about the isolation of the teacher's role. It also points to the existence of a set of agreed upon (but mistaken) teacher perceptions about parents. In other words the lack of a formal structure for teacher-teacher communication has not prevented the development of an informal network and the development of a teacher perspective. This informal network of communication centres on the staffroom. In the absence of the development of formal structures with a variety of purposes and means of communication it is likely that the staffroom would have remained an enclosed and relatively homogenous response by teachers to the outside world, with enormous power to influence the socialization of new teachers. A study carried out by Kelly (1970) in Dublin revealed that the parent–teacher relationships were characterized by hostility as well as misunderstanding.

> But before many Dublin teachers will accept that they have an educational duty to involve parents in the work of the school, a change in their definition of the teacher's role is necessary. It is unlikely that this will be easily achieved, as changes in socially defined role expectations are difficult to bring about and take time. Such change may have to overcome the hostility of both parents and teachers, and misunderstandings between them.
>   However, there are some signs of a desire for change among teachers. About half of the respondents said they would like to have more contact with parents, although some of this group of teachers foresaw difficulties in increasing parent-teacher contact ...

Changes in the teacher role have been forthcoming, even since 1968 when Kelly collected the data for the above paragraph. Relatively few of these changes have specifically affected the parent–teacher relationship. They have been associated with the differentiation and specialization within schools as schools have continued the trend towards becoming complex organizations, and they have been associated with the curriculum research and development movement that has developed new methods of communication both between schools and between schools and the academic community.

The following extract describing the organization of a comprehensive school illustrates a development in which new roles requiring new skills are required of teachers. The school is attempting a complex federation of autonomous units in an attempt to tackle the problems of size and co-ordination of effort. The result is an organizational and administrative structure far removed from 'the headmaster and a school secretary'.

The Federation has a formally differentiated authority structure with at least three dimensions:

administrative – including principal, heads of halls, director of studies, professional tutor.

academic – faculty heads and faculty members, and (with some faculties), subject heads and members.

pastoral – heads of hall, deputy heads of hall, senior tutors (who liaise with feeder schools) and all tutors in a hall.

The above is only one example of a number of developments within school organizations that are slowly transforming many aspects of the teacher's role.

The other aspect of the teacher's role mentioned earlier was the new relationship with curriculum development and research. In the 1950s, teachers could be left in isolation and uninterrupted in their classrooms because the academic subjects they taught held an unquestioned place in the curriculum. Similarly the method and content of their teaching was likely to go unchallenged, unless incompetent. The vast acceleration in the development of knowledge in universities and elsewhere and the rapid social change outside schools have affected this situation radically. Developments like the Schools Mathematics Project (SMP), designed to bring school mathematics into the twentieth century, contrast with the Humanities Curriculum Project (HCP) designed to change the teacher's role while introducing moral, political and social questions into the curriculum. But both are part of a multifaceted development that has brought methods of teaching and the content of the curriculum under the microscope as never before. The movement has brought together researchers, educationalists and teachers within development teams that have established new cross-organizational links. There have probably been in excess of 300 curriculum research and development projects (over 160 financed by the Schools Council alone) in the last twelve years. The relationships and roles developed within these and through the trial schools system which many of them use has not yet been studied. It is perhaps illustrative to quote from one project, the Reading Mathematics Project, a part of the philosophy of the evaluation, which is being undertaken by John Elliott.

In carrying out the evaluation, we shall aspire:

(1) *To be formative*. We aim to provide on-going feed-back about dissemination and implementation problems to those

who have some power to influence and help teachers' use of the project's ideas, e.g. the project director, disseminators, head teachers, local authority administrators, the Schools Council. We shall also make this information available to the teachers involved. In this way we hope the evaluation will support informed decisions.

(2) *To help disseminators and teachers in the task of self-evaluation.* The evaluation team will encourage disseminators and teachers to evaluate their own activities. Evaluation is seen as something everyone has a responsibilty for and not a specialist activity which can often be conducted by 'experts'. As 'outside evaluators', we view our role as fostering the capacity of all those involved in the dissemination and implementation of the project to evaluate their own practice. Our accounts of activities will be fed back, not as definitive statements, but as a stimulus for dialogue and discussion about problems and issues. Whenever possible, we shall ask for critiques of, and responses to, the reports we feed in and will then incorporate these into the evaluation reports in circulation.

(3) *To be democratic.* We shall try to monitor what happens as a result of dissemination. In doing so, we shall not only be concerned with the stated aims of the project to help teachers match learning experiences to the individual child, but we shall also be concerned with the full range of uses that others perceive the project to have. For example, some head teachers hope the project will foster communication between parents and teachers about children's learning requirements. Again, some LEA advisers hope it will help teachers in primary and middle schools to communicate with secondary school teachers at the transfer stage about the progress of pupils. The evaluation will aspire to be democratic in the sense that it will consider the interests of a variety of groups and not just those of the project developers.

This kind of relationship between the research and the teacher role will not be endorsed by all practising teachers. However, it does represent a development in which many teachers have taken part (Ruddock, 1976; Walker and Adelman, 1975; Elliott and MacDonald, 1975) and which has represented for many an extension of their role as teachers.

There are many other developments that could be described in this section to underline the major point that the teacher role is undergoing change at an unprecedented rate. For many the rate of change is too slow, for others it is in the wrong directions, and for many, I suspect a majority, it is too rapid and unsettling. These questions do not concern us here, we are more concerned to establish the fact and possibility of change. Unfortunately it is not a possibility often taken into account in the socialization of teachers.

Induction to the teacher role

The first or probationary year is one part of the teacher's career that has been extensively studied. Interest in this one year has been stimulated by the possibility of checking on the adequacy of the initial training and of extending training into this period. Unfortunately, the scatter of probationers in a variety of schools and the rather pragmatic focus of the investigations have given rise to a series of fact-finding questionnaire surveys that have contributed little to an understanding of the process of socialization of teachers. At the other end of the scale there have been a number of publications incorporating highly impressionistic reports, many of them autobiographical, from practising teachers (Hannam *et al*, 1976). These reports are often vivid and make good reading, but they usually fall short of giving background information and are too idiosyncratic to give a reliable picture.

It is not intended here to make an exhaustive review of these studies. A bibliography is included for this purpose. However, some of the findings do provide an important backcloth for the later chapters.

One of the early concerns of these investigators was to examine the continuity and relevance of training to the early teaching experience, in order to feed back the information to training courses. Some of the impetus for the reform of initial training has developed from these studies. Rudd and Wiseman (1962) surveyed teacher dissatisfaction and found that major 'sources of dissatisfaction apeared to be more related to factors in the teaching than those in the training situation' – for example, salaries, poor relationships, teaching loads, buildings and large classes. However, Wiseman and Start's (1965) follow-up study of nearly 250 teachers some five years after training pointed to considerable lack of continuity between grades obtained in training and later experience of promotion, satisfaction in teaching or even the headteacher's assessment of current work. This lack of continuity in the transition from training into practice will emerge as an important point later in the book. Less discontinuity was found in a study by Clark and Nisbet (1963), who found a small positive correlation between teaching practice assessment during training at Aberdeen College and an assessment made by inspectors nearly two years later (the end of the Scottish probation), but even here there are indications of strain and discontinuity. For instance, a third of the sample found teaching to be, at times, a strain on their health and difficulty with discipline emerged as a major problem.

A study by Cornwell (1965) of a large sample of Birmingham probationers produced evidence of another kind of discontinuity: over 30 per cent of secondary teachers found themselves teaching subjects for which they were not qualified and over 20 per cent were denied opportunity to teach subjects for which they were qualified. In addition over half the secondary teachers and nearly a third of primary teachers did not have a syllabus made available to them before the beginning of their first term. In these circumstances the discontinuity could have been very hard to surmount for some teachers who combined getting their syllabus late and teaching subjects for which they were not qualified. The survey included headteachers and pointed to some interesting discrepancies in perspective. Headteachers listed discipline as a major problem for probationers in 69 per cent of cases, whereas only 22 per cent of probationers saw this as a major problem. On the other hand probationers listed lack of equipment in 30 per cent of cases and lack of school policy in 20 per cent of cases. Headteachers differed considerably, with 19 per cent and 70 per cent respectively.

The headteachers' perspective	*The probationary teachers' perspective*
Lack of discipline and problems with backward children due to teaching methods, poor organization and preparation.	Problems with backward children due to poor equipment, inadequate buildings, lack of books, discipline, and lack of school policy.

The most extensive study in the field, by Taylor and Dale (1971), confirms many of the points already made. The percentages vary and in some cases this may indicate progress made in dealing with specific problems, for instance a larger proportion of teachers

46

state they receive a syllabus before term starts, but the picture is essentially similar. An interesting addition emerges in relation to the unsuccessful probationer whose probationary period is extended. Extension rates were higher in secondary than in primary schools and in those schools with a higher than average intake of children from 'difficult' neighbourhoods. In addition those probationers who taught in *urban* rather than rural schools who were not invited to an induction programme and who were working with an authority that was *not* their first choice, were also more likely to have their probation extended. A clear indication that factors increasing strain and discontinuity were contributing to failure in the probationary year. However, the proportions extended were very small (2–4 per cent) and the numbers who failed outright were almost negligible.

A final point, extracted from a mass of data, concerns the colleagues to whom the probationer turns for help and guidance about work. Taylor and Dale confirm Cornwell's finding that the 'headteacher' and 'an experienced colleague of own choice' are the people consulted most of the time (70 per cent). Cornwell, however, shows that in secondary schools the head is more distant and the experienced colleague and informal staffroom discussion rank well above the headmaster.

The emergence of an experienced colleague as an important influence on the probationary teacher is taken up in one of the few analytical studies of teacher socialization that seeks to test propositions about the process – a study of power and autonomy by Edgar and Warren (1969). This is an American study and not directly applicable to England, where evaluation by senior colleagues is less developed, but some of the conclusions are of interest if we bear in mind the higher degree of senior colleague evaluation in the American setting. Edgar and Warren studied attitude change over the first year of teaching of over 200 new teachers. In particular they were anxious to test the idea that new teachers would change their attitudes towards the views of a 'significant other' who was a senior colleague responsible for their evaluation. In addition they hoped to discover conditions which increase or decreased the effect. They summarize their results as follows:

1 'Organizational evaluation is a significant factor in professional socialization', i.e. new teachers do move towards the views of their evaluators.

2 'Personal liking between a teacher and his evaluator is a significant socialization variable', i.e. it increases the likelihood of the change in 1.
3 'Demands for autonomy often clash with existing attitudes of superiors.'
4 'Autonomy is more likely to be achieved by virtue of the teacher's resources or qualities rather than demand.'
5 'Satisfaction with teaching in general is related to satisfaction with the way tasks are allocated and evaluated.'
6 'New teachers want more control and guidance in such areas as discipline and clerical tasks and more autonomy in such areas as curriculum content and teaching methods.'

These findings dovetail closely with the research reported earlier. Young teachers see their major problems arising from discipline and difficult teaching assignments, that is, from the classroom. They depend for help on the formal structure of the school, the headmaster or senior colleague, but they turn equally to the friendly colleague, the person they like. Many find a lack of support facilities such as books and equipment and, more surprisingly, they feel a need, especially in some areas of work, for a clear school policy.

In addition to the research reported here there has been a considerable volume of work on the attitudes of student teachers and teachers in their probationary year. Work by McLeish (1970), Oliver (1965, 1968), Cope (1971), Cohen (1969) and Butcher (1965) will be drawn upon as the research data is analyzed in Chapters 3–5. The major finding of this research underlines the importance of the discontinuity between training and the reality of teaching. The attitudes of beginning teachers undergo dramatic change as they establish themselves in the profession, away from the liberal ideas of their student days towards the traditional patterns in many schools.

This change is complex and incomplete. Too much emphasis has been given to the obvious fact that the change occurs, and too little attention paid to the partial and incomplete nature of the change and the realization that new styles of teaching are emerging – not least because of the pressure and persistence of some of the younger teachers (Ashton *et al.* (1975)). We shall take up this theme again later.

Training

A decade ago the pattern of teacher training looked fixed within a gradually evolving tradition. It had an air of inevitability and neglect. It seemed doomed to be written about in terms so removed from the problems faced by many teachers in school that an observer could have been excused for thinking that the problems in schools had nothing to do with teacher training. Taylor (1969) quotes a good example:

> ... ways are open for intelligent modern people to achieve levels of insight which give meaning and dynamism to life, and which are integral to the growth of wholeness in persons, and to creative relationships between persons. For the educators of educators who are serious about life, and for whom the old landmarks have disappeared, there is the search for the timeless and living truth, which ...

As long ago as the 1930s, Waller (1932) wrote describing the training of teachers:

> The theory and the practice of education have suffered in the past from an over-attention to what ought to be and its correlative tendency to disregard what is. When theory is not based upon existing practice, a great hiatus appears between theory and practice, and the consequence of theory does not affect the conservatism of practice.

Waller is quick to point out the source of influence on young teachers:

> ... he gives up and takes his guidance from conventional sources, from advice of older teachers, the proverbs of the fraternity and the commandments of the principal.

Taylor (1969), writing specifically of colleges of education, criticizes them for 'suspicion of intellect', for 'a social and literary romanticism' which is combined with a 'hunger for the satisfaction of interpersonal life within the community and small group'. He accuses them of being over-concerned with consensus and culture and being insufficiently aware of conflict and structure. Taylor puts his faith in rationality and the rigour of academic discipline which characterizes the university approach to education. He voices his suspicion of amateurish synthesizing within the education courses in colleges.

The James Report (1972) took up this problem of 'dualism within the present system'.

> The concurrent form of training within the colleges of education suffers from a conflict and confusion of objectives. The colleges are required at one and the same time to extend for three years the personal education of the student and to train him as a teacher.

But James was less sanguine about the university's answer.

> Much of what has been said about the problems of three-year training also applies to the present arrangements for training graduates ... same proliferation of subject options ... too much emphasis on educational theory at expense of adequate preparation ... over-loading of initial programmes.

It is unlikely that the partial implementation of the James Report recommendations that have followed its publication will resolve the dilemma of academic discipline and professional preparation which underlies the discussion. The purposes of the brief analysis that follows is to indicate the direction of these changes and to introduce the empirical study on which most of the rest of the analysis is based.

Changes

The changes proposed by the James Report (1972) and the white paper, *A Framework for Expansion* (1972), have been overtaken by events. The falling birth rates of the early 1970s have persisted and given rise to a dwindling school population. Colleges that expanded rapidly in the 1960s are currently being cut back to prevent drastic over-production of teachers. The economic problems of 1975 and 1976 have led to cuts in local authority education budgets for the first time in the post-war years. Financial stringency has prevented the growth of in-service training anticipated by the James Report. Many of the changes affecting teacher education today have not, therefore, been brought about by a concern for the specific problems of teacher education. They derive from broad-based and deeply rooted sources within the demographic structures, economy and culture of our society.

In some respects these changes mirror the metamorphosis of teachers' colleges in the United States in the 1950s and 1960s studied by Roberts (1964). During this period locally financed, locally orientated teachers' colleges moved quickly to become state and regionally orientated institutions stressing a liberal education of general applicability. The basis of this new approach was the subject discipline. The increase in specialized areas of knowledge and the prestige of research within these disciplines meant that the whole thrust of the academic world cut across the organizational boundaries of the teachers' colleges. This relates to the criticisms of college culture voiced by Taylor (1969). In order to compete with universities in terms of prestige and outside recognition the colleges moved to emulate them.

> The modern teachers' college is gradually coming to be differentiated from non-professional colleges only by its low cost, its commuter nature, and by a few specialized professional requirements.

The recent mergers between colleges of education and polytechnics are producing institutions which are in many ways similar to those described by Roberts (1964) in the above quotation. We must examine the process within the English context.

The rapid expansion of teacher education has now been replaced by an even more rapid contraction. At the same time the DES has undertaken a complete restructuring of the institutional and course provision. Many colleges have been closed and many more will follow. A large number have been merged with other institutions, in particular polytechnics, and some have been allowed to remain independent. Within this changed institutional provision the course structure will also be changed. It will no longer be necessary for students entering higher education to make an early decision to teach. The first two years of the course will be a Diploma in Higher Education which will be a general, and for some terminal, qualification. Only at this point will it be necessary to opt finally for a professional qualification. The variety of courses negotiated between the colleges and the Council for National Academic Awards (CNAA) and/or the universities is immense, but it seems probable that the pattern that emerges will involve an all-graduate intake to the profession.

51

Clearly changes of this order and of this rapidity will have unpredictable effects on teacher socialization. Students who in the past had their training in small, stable institutions with a single-minded interest in the training of teachers will increasingly train in large cosmopolitan institutions. The staff of the small teacher training colleges will be scattered and it is highly unlikely that the traditional (prevailing) climate will be re-captured in the new institutions. Collier (1973) describes the way this process is perceived from the perspective of a college principal.

> The English tradition ... described by Butterfield ... 'a respect for the other man's personality, a recognition of what is due to political opponents, a certain homage to what the other man may think to be a political good ... without it democracy can only destroy itself in a conflict of divine right versus diabolical wrong' ... There is no doubt that the small size of educational institutions in England has reflected the high priority accorded to ... these clusters of values, and the trend towards larger schools and colleges is widely felt to be sacrificing something precious.

The institutions which replace them will in many cases be an amalgam of a number of traditions. Housed within a polytechnic with its own characteristic structure and climate, the education department consisting, in the main, of lecturers from the old college will nevertheless be drastically reorganized. The principal will lose the all-embracing power so characteristic of the college. The new men and women in positions of authority will be influenced by a new range of constraints and uncertainties. Many of them will re-train and bring new skills to the new situation.

The outcome of this change is not predictable with any precision. In fact, a major concern for those interested in the question that we are examining will be to study the changes that take place as soon as they can be recognized and characterized. It will tell us a great deal about the (changing) relationship between the individual and the social institution – the central concern of this book. What can be predicted is that the process of rapid change within the teaching profession is likely to be accelerated. The sort of changes taking place within schools will now be mirrored by those taking place in teacher training institutions. They can be presented as follows:

Table 2.5

Traditional	Emergent
small	large
simple administrative structure	complex administrative structure
local	cosmopolitan
intake selected on professional bases	broader, non-selected intake
general, non-specialist curriculum	more specialist
paternalistic authority style	managerial authority style

It is in this broad context of change in the training of teachers that teacher socialization should be examined.

The research

The research into teacher socialization described in this book is one aspect of a broader study which included an evaluation of the Sussex University school-based method of teacher training. The evaluation, which was a comparative study and is written up in the Tutorial Schools Project Report (1973), is not reported here, although some data from the comparative study are presented if they illustrate the socialization process.

The major elements of the Sussex school-based innovation are reported here so that the descriptions that follow can be placed in their social context. The scheme was developed in the mid-sixties in response to the criticisms of teacher training, in particular, the separation of theory and practice and the lack of effective co-operation between schools and university departments of education. The innovation was one of the first and most radical in the field but it has been followed by a growing number of changes in PGCE courses throughout the country. The main elements of the innovation can be summarized as follows:

(1) In order to link the school and University in a close relationship, the traditional bloc teaching practice (one term or six week periods) was changed. The students now spent three days per week for the whole year within the school.

(2) To support the students within the school, a teacher-tutor was appointed from among the teaching staff and paid a small fee to give weekly tutorials to two students in his own subject. The tutor became responsible for the assessment

of their teaching practice. Since a school might receive more than one pair of students, a general supervisory tutor was appointed to co-ordinate the efforts of the teacher-tutors and give fortnightly seminars to a much larger group of students on problems affecting the school.

(3) The school-university link became the responsibility of an education tutor (E-tutor) who was a joint appointment between the Education Area of the University and one of the subject groups in the Arts or Science Areas of the university. The E-tutor visited schools, ran a subject workshop during the Autumn Term and convened a joint seminar with students and teacher-tutors during the Spring Term.

(4) The rest of the course, seminars in values, sociology and psychology, were undertaken by university staff. The course was examined through the students' work-file and an assessment of teaching practice on a pass-fail basis.

(5) One intended element of the innovation did not become part of the established course. It had been hoped that student, teacher-tutor teams within the school would act as a milieu for training and as a resource for experimentation. For example, in the final term the students might take over most of the teaching from the teacher-tutor and enable him to attend the University to develop new aspects of his pedagogy or subject discipline. Very few tutors ever made use of this negotiated right. We shall see that the failure of this element of the scheme resulted from an underestimation of the difficulty of bringing about inter-institutional co-operation and of the differences in university and school culture. These differences affected the working of other aspects of the scheme and the socialization of beginning teachers.

Conclusion

This chapter has covered a wide area and has touched on a number of the most important aspects of teaching under the headings: the career, the role and the induction process. When teaching was examined as a career it was found to include a number of career strands. Not all the strands can be examined within this book and there is a particular emphasis on graduate teacher careers. Within this restricted area, sub-strands of the teaching career are discernible, for example with respect to sex differences.

An examination of the teachers' role revealed a similar lack of unity and an additional lack of consensus. Not only were there differences in the concept of the role (for example traditional versus progressive) but the scope and context of the role was shown to be changing as schools become complex organizations.

Induction into teaching is probably the most studied aspect of the teacher's career. The studies reviewed in this chapter were in agreement upon a number of important points. The discontinuity between training to become a teacher and the first job as a teacher was expressed in a number of studies and explored in a number of ways; also important was the difference of perspective within the school between the probationary teacher and the headmaster.

The chapter concludes by examining the training of teachers and the effect of recent changes within teacher training. While the detailed administrative and academic results of the reorganization and cut back of teacher training are still uncertain the general direction of the change is more easily predictable.

The chapter is intended to provide a backcloth against which the more detailed analysis of teacher socialization given in the following chapter can be seen and gain in relevance. Teacher education is proceeding within a context in which the scale and complexity of organizations is increasing and the rate of change is accelerating. The uncertainties and conflicts in the profession are likely to be augmented. It is against this background that we must approach the study of teacher socialization.

Chapter 3

We have seen that the student teacher has come to teaching from a variety of backgrounds. We have sketched some of the major patterns of their careers and have indicated how possessing certain initial characteristics influences their expected career. We have seen that major changes are taking place in the structure of schools and in the role of the teacher and that these are paralleled by changes in many of the training institutions. What is missing from the account is an examination of the process through which induction into teaching comes about. What does this process mean for individuals? How do they perceive it? What does it feel like to go through it? Finally, in line with our concern for the sociology of the possible, what can an individual or group do to obtain some control over certain features of the process?

The account that follows is a descriptive, analytical study of the graduate teacher training year at Sussex University. It will provide us in the first phase of the analysis with a conceptual framework for a more general discussion of teacher socialization. The account is derived from a study which used both participant observation and questionnaire techniques. The fieldwork techniques interacted with the building of a theoretical model in a way that conformed fairly closely with that described by Barney Glaser and Anselm Strauss (1968) as 'grounded theory':

Most writing on sociological method has been concerned with how accurate facts can be obtained and how theory can thereby be more rigorously tested ... we address ourselves to the equally important enterprise of how the discovery of theory from data – systematically obtained and analyzed in social research – can be furthered. We believe that the discovery of theory from data – which we call grounded theory – is a major task confronting sociology today, for, as we shall try to show, such a theory fits empirical situations, and is understandable to sociologists and layman alike. Most important, it works – provides us with relevant predictions, explanations, interpretations and applications.

In particular this meant that the dominant direction of analysis was from the data, collected in a variety of ways, towards the generation of concepts that proved useful in 'making sense' of that data. Where possible the sequence of events, observations and analysis, has been made clear in the narrative.

As we have seen the Sussex Post-Graduate Certificate had an unusual structure. Students were expected to teach in schools for three days a week throughout the year. Their work in school was supervised by a teacher-tutor, who was appointed from among the staff of the teaching practice school. The teacher-tutor was expected to arrange tutorials with his two students. As there was usually more than one teacher-tutor in a school the overall supervision and co-ordination of the students' school experience was located with a general supervisory tutor, who was often the headmaster. It was hoped that this arrangement would ensure that the help and advice the student needed with the finer points of teaching would be given by someone who had close contact with the children being taught. At the university the student attended two major seminar series, a subject-discipline based seminar and a social science/philosophy seminar. The former were run by education tutors (E-tutors) and the latter by a mixture of sociologists, psychologists, philosophers and others; the latter seminars were attended by students from a variety of subject backgrounds.

As part of my research plan I attended a cross section of seminars of both varieties. In each year the subject seminars I attended covered both arts and science, for example, the history and physical sciences seminars in 1969–70 and the biology and English seminars in 1970–71. I also spent a lot of time talking to students informally and visiting them in their teaching schools.

As I spent my time listening and talking to students two broad areas of concern recurred within their conversations. One was the problem of becoming a teacher. As an outsider I had forgotten and underestimated the uncertainties, doubts and tensions felt by students as they wrestled with problems of classroom control, the presentation of their subject to children and their relationships with established teachers. The second characteristic that surprised me was the extent to which the students' previous undergraduate experience shaped and influenced their reaction to the course and their fellow students.

The following quotations were recorded by me in a variety of situations. They were by no means atypical:

'I don't know how I would justify teaching French. It's one of those competitive subjects.' (English student)
'Facts, that's all they (the scientists) have to offer. We are the only group that are concerned about education.' (English student)
'This is really an arts course.' (Science student)
'Then I heard someone behind me say "Why do you have to keep quoting books, can't you think for yourself?", and I felt really good because there was another science student with some commonsense.' (Science student)

It became very clear that while students came from a variety of home backgrounds, with a wide range of commitment to being teachers and from a large number of universities, one of the characteristics that most coloured their early reaction to the course was the subject specialization of their first degree. Scientists, for example, tended to react to the 'creativity' sessions by complaining that they 'had not come on the course to learn to paint and cut up cardboard' and that the sessions were 'a waste of time'. The primary and English students, on the other hand, were most enthusiastic about these sessions, claiming that they produced 'just the release I required from the set patterns of thinking acquired in my degree course' and that 'it was valuable experience to know what a child feels like when you present it with a blank sheet of paper and ask it to write a poem'.

It became apparent that many of the questions raised in the different subject groups concerned similar problems, for example discipline and homework but they were frequently posed in a different context and in a different 'language'. In addition, many of the questions arose from concerns that were specific to particular subject groups. For example, the English group became concerned with fundamental problems of 'what is English?', or 'what is the role of the teacher?', while the scientists were far more likely to shy from this type of problem and take up issues like, 'how does one teach osmosis or the periodic table?'.

These subject group differences were clearly established in my mind by the time the questionnaire data was ready for analysis. It was an obvious step therefore to see if the differences in student academic culture that I had observed in seminars and in conversation were reflected in attitudes, as measured by our questionnaires. I chose generalized attitude measures to test my observations because I did not want the different teaching contexts and teaching styles associated with the subjects to directly affect the results.

The measures were chosen because they included important attitudes, relevant to educators and social scientists. The three scales presented here were developed by R. A. C. Oliver and H. J. Butcher in the 1950s and widely used in the late 1960s and 70s in research into teachers' attitudes. Several other scales were used in the research but are not reported here to avoid overcomplicating the presentation.

Naturalism Naturalism presumes the existence of natural standards that reside within the child and emerge in a relationship with the child. It is therefore opposed to the imposition of external (absolute) standards in the moral, cultural or academic sphere. Agreement with items like 'naturalness is more important than good manners in children' and 'the teacher should not stand in the way of a child's efforts to learn in his own fashion' is balanced by disagreement with items like 'character training is impossible if there is no formal standard of right or wrong' to score positively for Naturalism.

Radicalism Radicalism is concerned with the allocation of resources to and the distribution and availability of education. In general, more education, more equally distributed is at the centre of the concept. For example, agreement with 'more nursery schools', 'increased expenditure on adult education' and 'comprehensive schools to be the normal form of secondary education' would score positively on the Radicalism scale.

Tendermindedness Tendermindedness is *against* narrowly conceived vocationalism and instrumentalism in education and is *against* efficiency in fitting children into the 'system'. It is therefore a very negative concept and can only be conceived of as protecting children from demands of the future and the 'system'. The tenderminded person would be against 'a scientific training offers good prospects for a career' as a reason for teaching science and against 'a study of international affairs should show which countries are our friends' as a reason for teaching international understanding.

In other words, 'a tenderminded attitude to education is one which regards children and others as persons to be treated as ends in themselves rather than as serving the interests of others, as represented, for example, by the demands of vocational efficiency or the interests of the State'.

An inspection of the means for the seven subject or specialist groups on the three scales showed a heartening degree of consistency between them and more importantly a variation between subject groups which closely paralleled the observation data. For example, the English and primary groups scored higher than the physics/chemistry and maths groups on each scale. Interestingly the comments about the French student teachers that I recorded in the English group are consistent with the low scores recorded by the French students on each of the three scales. In the table below the means have been used to establish a rank order for each scale.

Table 3.1 *Mean rank ordering of subject groups on N, R and T scales*

	Naturalism	Radicalism	Tender-mindedness	Mean Rank
English	1	1	2	1·3
Primary	2	3	3	2·7
Biology	4	4	1	3·0
History	3	2	5	3·3
Maths	5	6	4	5·0
French	7	5	7	6·3
Physics/Chem.	6	7	6	6·3

Source: TSRP (1973)

In addition when the questionnaire data for other universities was examined there were broad similarities in the pattern with

the English, primary and social science groups recording high
scores and the physical sciences low scores.

Subject sub-cultures

In describing the essential elements of student sub-culture
Howard Becker (1961) was strongly influenced by Albert Cohen
(1955) when he wrote:

> Sub-cultures develop when a number of people are faced with
> common problems and interact both intensively and exten-
> sively in the effort to find solutions for them. This intensive
> interaction in an isolated group produces a particularly mean-
> ingful and essential array of those understandings and agree-
> ments we call student culture.

It was quite clear from my observations and the questionnaire
data that I had examined that students from particular subject
disciplines exhibited an array of 'understanding and agreements'.
What I could not be sure about was how 'meaningful and
essential' they were and how important they were in delineating
sub-groups within the broader student culture. Two sources of
evidence contributed to my understanding of this issue.

During a period of observation of 'English' students in schools,
I was told that some 'French' students also took odd English
lessons. Almost casually I decided to sit in. The 'French' students
approached the teaching of English as they would a foreign
language, using comprehension exercises, question and answer
techniques and 'complete the sentence' exercises. Predominant in
their approach was the notion that English represented a body of
rules and meanings that had to be transmitted authoritatively by
the teacher. Later on, I observed other 'French' students and
teachers teaching French and confirmed this observation. Among
the 'English' students there existed a second view, in part complementary but also challenging the above approach. This can
be summarized as the notion that English represented the means
of expression of the children in the class and that a major task of
the teacher was to facilitate the use of that means of expression.
This frequently meant that the teacher attempted to generate a
relaxed and informal atmosphere in the classroom so that communication was not inhibited and the child felt motivated to
express himself.

This example of differences in teaching style of students shows

61

that the differences noticed in the university permeate the schools and in some cases even affect the classroom behaviour of students.

The second source of information on this issue was obtained from a sociometric questionnaire administered at York and Sussex. It is to be expected that shared cultural elements will be reflected in friendship patterns developed during the course, and if those elements coincide with an emerging perspective, relevant to teaching, they will remain strong for the duration of the course. In other words, if a biologist really does feel at home with biologists, he will tend to choose his friends from among them, rather than other students. The evidence from the end of year sociometric questionnaire bore this out.

Table 3.2 *Percentage of friendship choices made within own subject group*

	Sussex	York
Closest friend choice	78%	79%
3 closest friends	68%	78%
All friends (up to 6 named)	60%	67%

At Sussex, 60 per cent of the total number of friends chosen come from within the chooser's own subject group. If the closest friend only is taken as an indicator, then the percentage is 78 per cent within the subject group, indicating that, the *more* important the friendship, the *more* likely they are to be chosen from the subject group. This finding is confirmed at York, where 67 per cent of friends and 79 per cent of closest friends are chosen from within subject groups.

Some idea of the significance of this finding or its meaning in terms of relationships can be got from comparing the in-group solidarity of these subject groups with pupils in a grammar school. The grammar school organized the entire day, 9 a.m. to 4 p.m., around class units. A pupil entering the school in the morning would, after registration, be taught in a class which rarely altered in its composition throughout the day. Enclosed in this tight organizational framework the second year pupils made 58 per cent of their friendship choices within the classroom. This was well above the randomly expected level of 25 per cent. However, the rigid organizational framework of the grammar school contrasts with the loose open structure of the PGCE course. The extent to which these post-graduate students select friends from their own subject must on a first impression seem surprisingly high and be regarded as evidence of the appropriateness of the term subject sub-cultures, to describe the phenomena that we are examining.

It is important to stress that this result cannot be explained simply by the organizational arrangements of the course. Activities that caused student-teachers to meet in subject homogeneous groups were about as frequent as activities that caused them to meet in mixed subject groups. When the effect of the mixed subject groups on friendship choice was examined, in the same way as for the subject groups, they were found to have little effect.

Table 3.3 *Effects of seminar groups (mixed subjects) on friendship choices*

	% of friendship choices made by members of group to other members of group	% of member to member choices expected by chance
Sussex		
1. Sociology + Psychology Groups	16	11–12
2. Creativity + Values Groups	15	
York		
1. Philosophy seminars	25	25

While the Sussex seminars seemed to have slight effects on student friendship choices, the York groupings seemed to have no effect at all. At neither university do these groupings have anything approaching the effect of the subject groups.

The effect of sharing the same teaching practice school was also examined and although it affected which students were chosen as friends it did not affect the proportion of students chosen from outside the students' own subject discipline. They remained a minority.

The subject sub-culture appears therefore to be a pervasive phenomenon, affecting a student-teacher's behaviour in school and university, as well as their choice of friends and their attitudes towards education. It would seem there is a case for considering the process of becoming a teacher as a multi-stranded process in which subject sub-culture insulate the various strands from one another. In other words while it is readily accepted that subject disciplines enhance understanding and communication it is often forgotten that between subject disciplines there can be a gulf in which misunderstanding, categorization and prejudice or simply lack of interest and concern, may develop.

McLeish (1970) working with a large sample of college students and lecturers confirmed the importance of this finding.

> The most remarkable differences in attitudes of any in the total sample appear to be between subject-specialists. These are certainly more significant than the differences due to political or religious affiliations. Similar differences to those found in the students on entry to their courses are found as between college lecturers specializing in these 'main' subjects.

Our own data later confirmed that differences between subject specialists occurred just as markedly in schools and affected the patterns of association between students and school teachers.

Situationally constrained strategies

The effect of developing the concept of subject sub-cultures was to provide me, the observer, with a crude conceptual framework against which I could examine the 'talk' I listened to. Much of what I heard confirmed my ideas on the importance of subject sub-cultures, but increasingly as I participated in a wider range of group activities, the events I observed challenged my understandings.

I noticed that mixed subject discipline seminars were more formal and tense than seminars containing only one subject group. This confirmed a lack of communication between subject sub-cultures. However, in addition to this I noticed that individuals whom I knew quite intimately within their subject group sometimes behaved rather differently in a mixed seminar. For example, a biologist who played what could be described as a 'progressive' role in the biology seminar, advocating child-centred techniques and liberal educational reforms, became an advocate of formal academic standards and firm discipline within the mixed seminar. When I questioned him on this reversal, he found it difficult to accept that it had occurred, until I was able to detail the statements he had made and the context of the discussions. He resolved the problem after much perplexed heart-searching by remarking that, within the mixed seminar there were a couple of primary students 'who really get my goat'. It appeared to him that they were unrealistic in their outlook and needed bringing back to earth. It became apparent that he felt that the biologists in his subject group were different. He could rely on their commonsense and understand their outlook and problems. He therefore felt free to espouse progressive causes in the biology seminar.

The important point to notice is that the biology student decided which strategy was appropriate to each seminar and it was his appraisal of the situation in each seminar that gave rise to the change in behaviour. My own external view of the mixed seminar had not been sufficient for me to interpret the change.

In other words, although the student composition of the seminar became a situational determinant of behaviour, giving rise to two recognizable and different strategies, it did not do so in any direct and automatic sense. This case illuminated two elements in the situation. It confirmed the existence of a set of understood values and orientations existing within the biology group (a subject sub-culture) and not among the mixed group of students. And it emphasized the importance of the student's interpretation of that situation and his ability to choose distinctive social strategies. This pointed to the necessity for modifying and elaborating the simple, rather deterministic model that had emerged.

The analysis has taken us back to the point at which we began this book: to the search for a less deterministic framework in which to study socialization. Interestingly, the idea on which it appears possible to build such a framework is contained in the notion of social strategy used earlier.

Let us consider the steps by which the deficiency in the original model was realized.

The observation of the contrasting strategies did not allow the observer to interpret why they had occurred until, firstly, it was clear the biology student recognized that specific differences between the biology and mixed groups existed. Secondly, it was clear that he intended to do something about establishing a balance which he saw as missing within the mixed seminar, particularly, counteracting the 'unrealistic' arguments of the primary students.

The observer had to know something about (1) the student's interpretation of the situation and (2) his purpose.

The incident with the biology student and my analysis of it led me to look out for more evidence of contrasting strategies, developed by individual students, to deal with the differing situations in which they found themselves. It was not long before I obtained examples that illustrated many other types of differential constraint. For example I observed and compared behaviour within seminars and behaviour outside seminars; behaviour within the classroom and behaviour in the staffroom; behaviour within the university and behaviour within schools.

At the same time I looked for evidence in the literature that other sociologists had dealt with the problem I faced. Like many problems in sociology there was a substantial theoretical literature with which I was already familiar. Starting with writers like G. H. Mead in the thirties and proceeding through Dennis Wrong's article (1961) on the oversocialized conception of man, there was a broad strand of symbolic interactionist and phenomenological writing with which I had much sympathy. Unfortunately there were few empirical studies that had developed a revelant conceptual framework. The field was reduced even further if one added the criteria that the conceptual framework had been worked out within a grounded theory approach. The work that came closest to this was research carried out by Howard Becker, Blanche Geer and Everett Hughes (1961) on medical students.

Even within these studies there were two important, and related, points of difference with the present work. First, Becker and his team had stressed the homogeneity of student culture, secondly they had stressed the pervasive and determining influence of the formal university structure. I came to different conclusions on both these issues but have nevertheless leaned heavily on Becker's use of concepts like culture, latent culture and perspective in developing the theoretical framework in the account that follows.

On the question of a student culture Becker wrote: 'Whether one sees one student culture or many on a campus is partly a matter of the researcher's choice.' The use of the term 'partly' makes it impossible to disagree with this statement. The use of 'partly' also obscures the issue because it is the other part of the procedure that is important. It is not sufficient simply to state '... students seem to us to be very much alike. We have found it more useful to think and talk about one student culture than to think about many student cultures'. It is necessary to generate and examine evidence of the homogeneity or heterogeneity of student culture. In this book we have examined evidence about subject subcultures because of the importance of making an *informed* judgment about them in relation to the process of becoming a teacher.

Becker expresses the lack of differentiation in student perspectives indirectly as well as directly. His constant references to 'the students' and 'student perspectives' gives his reader the impression of unity and wholeness without Becker having to muster a supporting argument. The clearest illustration of this technique occurs in *Boys in White* (1961). When describing the way faculty influence student perspectives he writes: 'The faculty and administration have a tremendous amount of power over the students and, in principle, can control student activities very tightly and cause students to act in whatever fashion they (the faculty) want. To the degree that the faculty actually exercises such power, students will have no opportunity to build their own perspectives and will simply take over ideas formed on them by the faculty ...'

It is clear from this quotation that the lack of emphasis on the possibility of differentiation becomes linked in Becker's analysis with the lack of student autonomy in the development of perspectives.

The lack of student autonomy expressed here by Becker is both surprising and worrying. There is clearly a need for an additional concept that expresses the autonomy of the individual in the face of coercive social pressures as the term 'anti-group sub-culture' developed in my analysis of student cultures in *Hightown Grammar* (1970) expresses the possibility of autonomous subcultural developments within a parent culture. The term I propose for this purpose is 'social strategy'.

The term 'strategy' is appropriate because it implies a purposive, guiding, autonomous element, within individual and group behaviour. It is clear that the uniformities in human behaviour, which give rise to recognizable patterns in research, indicate that individual social strategies for the most part comply with or are modified by constraining social forces. The implication here is that the constraints of the situation and the *individual's purpose* within that situation must be taken into account.

A social strategy is reducable to actions and ideas but it is only interpretable in the context of a specific situation. A social strategy involves the act or in the selection of ideas and actions and working out their complex interrelationships (action-idea systems) in a given situation. The selection of these action-idea systems as a student moves from situation to situation, need not be consistent. For example, the student may select a permissive action-idea system for a university seminar but an authoritarian one for a school classroom. The justification for this change might be a consciously thought out argument or it can be suppressed. In the first case, the social strategy is conscious, in the second case sub-conscious. The apparent contradiction in the selection of social strategies can only be resolved by reference to the student and his changing view of what represents the 'real' world and his relationship to it. I can illustrate this by referring to a commonly occurring series of events experienced by the students we studied.

The first time the student teacher uses an authoritarian strategy within the classroom, shouting, threatening or demanding order, he or she often sees it as a last resort, a temporary solution and not 'really them'. They frequently report viewing themselves from outside. 'Was that really me? It was horrible.' As the student resorts more and more frequently to this strategy, he or she needs more and more to justify its use and to rehearse the arguments with others to obtain reassurance and support.

The frequent resort to a particular social strategy, colours the perception and world view of the student and eventually the qualified teacher. The model being constructed here envisages a state of constant flux; constant competition between individuals in the selection of strategies and a changing balance. The individual is in a constant dialogue with himself about his position. An apparently static position is only obtained through achieving a balance in this dynamic system. The individual produces a constant formula for using certain strategies in certain situations and rejecting others. The precariousness of this balance can be demonstrated by studying changes in apparently stable personalities when their position within a social system changes abruptly.

Socialization is here presented as a constant flow of choices facing an individual. The position of an individual at any given time is like the position of a canoeist on fast-flowing rapids. He can only hold the canoe in a stable position by expending a considerable amount of energy and constantly making many judgements and choices about his course of action. Our cohort of students is like a large batch of canoeists all setting out together on the rapids, learning the skills as they attempt to find some quiet water and stabilize their position. *They are doing this in competition with other canoeists and must bear their competitors in mind in the selection of strategies for survival and success.*

In our discussion so far we have used the terms culture, sub-culture, perspective and social strategy. It is now time to clarify them and see their inter-relationships.

We have already examined Becker's definition of culture with its emphasis on 'common problems' and the possibility of 'intensive interaction' to produce solutions. Becker gives us an alternative definition of culture which links the concepts of culture and perspective.

> When we speak of student culture, we refer to a set of understandings shared by students and a set of actions congruent with those understandings. Student culture, from this point of view, is a shared way of looking at one's world and acting in it. To use other words, it is a set of perspectives on one's situation. This, of course, is one of the possible meanings of *culture*. In adding the qualifying adjective *student* to culture we mean to indicate that the understandings and actions grow up around the student's role as a student – they are specific to the student role.

Becker is not always clear about the way sub-cultures aggregate to form a culture and the way perspectives contribute to make up a culture. I think it becomes clearer if we realize that the common elements of solutions generated by individual students to solve their own problems have a life outside the situation. Because once a student knows that a problem facing him has been solved by others in a particular way it influences his search for a solution. Once developed these solutions contribute to the constraints in other similar situations. The more these solutions are copied and accepted as the way to solve problems the more they become an unchallenged part of social life. Perspectives exist on a different level of generalization and development to the idea of culture. Perspective describes a stage in the development of culture. Becker gets close to this in the following quotation (Hughes, Becker and Geer, 1958):

> The student's interpretation of specific events and issues tends to be made in categories that are part of the *student culture* ... It is not that the student must abide by these informal and

hardly conscious agreements, but rather that they *constrain* his thinking and *perspective* almost without his being aware of it ...

(my emphasis)

We can now see that sub-culture differs from perspective because sub-culture is simply a variant of the total culture, a sub-division at about the same level of generalization. It is a heuristic sub-division of the term culture and needs no separate definition.

The link between sub-cultures, perspectives and social strategies can now be spelled out.

As a group of individuals develop or acquire a sense of common purpose, so the sets of strategies adopted by them acquire a common element. It is this common element that enables the common perspective to emerge. As the perspective develops, and if over a long period of time, the situations that continually face the group have a common element, then the understandings broaden and develop to produce a sub-culture. The mark of the sub-culture is that its most important elements are not immediately lost if the individual leaves the group and the common situation of the group members. Perspectives are more quickly taken up and dropped than sub-cultures. To be sure the elements of sub-culture are often suppressed and can be almost completely covered by later behaviour patterns but the supposition here is that these elements effect changes deep within the personality structure of the individual and are responsible for the richness, complexity and uniqueness of individual personality. Jackson and Marsden (1962) have illustrated the way in which some upwardly mobile working-class pupils suppress, compensate for or react against their working-class culture. Becker has expressed the position of individuals who leave one sub-culture and enter a new activity, as possessing a 'latent culture', that is 'the culture has its origin and social support in a group other than the one in which the members are now participating'. The individual takes with him characteristics of the previous group, which are *potential*. They need to be developed to provide social strategies in the new setting. This is a valuable idea, and one that will be used in the description of student-teacher socialization that follow. It is important to tie the idea of 'latent culture' in with the concept of social strategy. Latent culture provides the basis for but also limits the number of strategies available to an individual in any given situation. For example, a scientist student-teacher is unlikely to be able to impress a mixed seminar which includes a number of student-teachers who are arts graduates, with his breadth of reading in literature. Depending on how markedly the latent culture or subculture limits social strategies and how difficult these limitations are to overcome, there will be a simple or a complex array of perspectives in the new institution. In situations, such as a school where social class is a latent culture, working-class pupils will have a limited choice of strategies and the limitations will be difficult to overcome.

The active, creative ingredient introduced into the model of adult socialization described here is dependent on the idea of individual purpose contained in the notion of social strategy. Individuals compete within situations in selecting and implementing favoured strategies. There can be no completely homogeneous response in a normal situation because as soon as one individual makes a move, the situation has changed and some options are now less satisfactory than others to the remaining members of the group. If, for example, in a classroom one pupil shows he has done all the learning and knows all the answers, some pupils will begin to see that competition along these lines (a 'good pupil' strategy) is not likely to succeed. Others may feel there is still some point in competing. The continuation of interaction produces a differentiation of strategies. The identification of a person with a strategy or set of strategies causes some stability in the process. The attachment of the individual to his reputation becomes a factor in the choice of future strategies. There is a sense in which differentiation and common understanding proceed together, for while the pupils are being identified with the strategies they choose, they are also developing common perspectives as pupils because they all adopt strategies that are recognizably appropriate to pupils. The innovation of new strategies complicates the picture at this point. Some innovations are immediately defined as inappropriate and the pupil expelled or punished, others become part of a changing array of recognized, although by no means equally valued strategies, available to subsequent cohorts of pupils.

I have criticized Becker for failing to provide a conceptual framework in which this differentiation is given the prominence it deserves. The importance of this omission is underlined when we consider social change and the way Becker fails to see in the process of adult socialization a potent source of change in institutions. Becker's construction of socialization frees man from enslavement to his past, from a determinism based on personality, 'some unchanging components in the self or personality', but instead enslaves him to the present, 'the individual turns himself into the kind of person the situation demands' (Becker, 1971). According to Becker institutions remain stable with change being handed down from the top and cohorts are socialized by the process of 'situational adjustment'. As he expresses it:

> Situations occur in institutions: stable institutions provide stable situations in which little change takes place. When the institutions themselves change, the situations they provide for their participants shift and necessitate development of new patterns of belief and action. When, for instance, a university decides to up-grade its academic programme and begins to require more and different kinds of work from its students, they must adjust to the new contingencies with which the change confronts them. (14)

Adjustment of this sort in which the individual is constantly transforming himself into 'the kind of person the situation demands' is only one part of the process of adult socialization. It may be the most important part in the process, but that is an empirical question. I intend for the purpose of this chapter to subsume 'situational adjustment' under the broader heading of 'social strategy'. It becomes a variety of social strategy. Two varieties of situational adjustment are readily recognizable:

1 Strategic compliance, in which the individual complies with the authority figure's definition of the situation and the constraints of the situation but retains private reservations about them. He is merely seen to be good.
2 Internalized adjustment, in which the individual complies with the constraints and believes that the constraints of the situation are for the best. He really is good.

Social strategies also include action-idea systems that are innovative within situations and change them. These innovations can be small scale and idiosyncratic or collective and large scale, in which case quite large scale institutional changes can take place. As Blumer (1966) wrote: 'With the mechanism of self-interaction, the human being ceases to be a responding organism whose behaviour is a product of what plays upon him from the outside, the inside or both. Instead, he acts towards his world interpreting what confronts him and organising his action on the basis of the interpretation.'

Social strategies are, therefore, selected or created and guided by a wide range of factors including, as we have seen, the individual's interpretation of the situation, but one factor that must not be neglected is *the ability of the performer*. A good performance can result in a strategy being acceptable in a situation where it had previously been unacceptable. The idea of adjustment to the situation overlooks one important point. As far as the organization is concerned the situation is usually 'defined' according to the *interpretation* of the organizationally most powerful person taking a part in the social drama.

This person can be and often is influenced in making his interpretation by the quality of the performance.

Strategic redefinition of the situation implies that change is brought about by individuals who do not possess the formal power to do so. They achieve change by causing or enabling those with formal power to change their interpretation of what is happening in the situation. This final category of social strategy is not meant to provide an exhaustive classification. It is intended to redress the balance in the literature. Let us return to the teaching profession to consider the importance of this type of strategy. While it must be recognized that student-teachers have no formal power to change schools they do possess important advantages in employing redefinition strategies. For example, teacher-tutors frequently mentioned that they were pleased to have Sussex students in their schools because the students brought with them up to date ideas in their subject and new ideas about ways of teaching it. The teacher-tutors also frequently pointed to the importance to them of having to rethink their ideas about their own teaching methods in order to explain them to the students. Several tutors mentioned that they had got into a rut and having students had helped them to realize it. One or two mentioned that the students had enabled them to try out new ideas that they had been waiting to try for several years. They had been unable to do so because of lack of resources within the school. For these tutors experiments in small group teaching only became possible when the two students arrived from the university.

An important final point to note is that the introduction of the concept of social strategy changes the weight carried by the Becker concept of perspective. Recognizable, action-idea systems now fall within the concept of social strategy. Perspective takes on a meaning much closer to its dictionary definition 'relation in which parts of subject are viewed by the mind, view, prospect'.

The following list outlines the changes that have been made to Becker's conceptual farmework.

Table 3.4

Becker *et al*.	Redefinition for this study
Culture	Definition accepted.
Sub-culture	Difference with culture made explicit – used to illuminate the sub-cultural differentiation of student culture on subject discipline lines.
Latent culture	Definition accepted.
Perspective	Accepted but modified to exclude action.
Situational perspective	Accepted but once again the 'action' outcomes are excluded.
Social strategy – not used.	New concept developed to include 'action' and 'purpose' of actor.
Situational adjustment	Accepted but subsumed under social strategy as a type of strategy – also sub-divided into strategic compliance and internalized adjustment.
Strategic redefinition – not used	New concept. Another sub-type of social strategy in which the actor is active in changing the socializing institution.

Quite clearly the process of acceptance and redefinition of these concepts proceeded slowly during the period of fieldwork and analysis. The emergence of the concept of social strategy, however, did come early enough in the research for some questionnaire items to be designed to examine the way student-teachers dealt with contrasting situations, for example, of the kind that gave rise to the biology students' apparently inconsistent behaviour. In one question they were asked how they dealt with situations in which differences existed between their E-tutor at the university and their teacher-tutor at the school. These strategies are looked into in some detail in the next chapter but it is useful to illustrate the conscious use of strategic compliance strategies in order to give flesh to the theoretical account. The following quotations are extracted from the questionnaires:

Often it wasn't worth bringing conflict with teacher-tutor to a head, since there was a definite non-communication and it was a waste of precious school time. It was more useful and peaceful to go away and do your own thing quietly.

The teacher-tutor was, of necessity, more in favour of audio–visual methods than the E-tutor. This simply meant that in practical terms one used those aspects of the method in class that produced the best response and discussed the philosophical impossibility of the entire exercise with the E-tutor.

These quotations will be examined again in the context of a descriptive analysis of the process of becoming a teacher but at this point they do serve to illustrate the resilience and the sophistication of the individual faced with conflicting institutional pressures. We can now express the process of change from student to student-teacher status using the concepts developed in this chapter.

I have suggested that the student's involvement with his subject goes much deeper than that usually implied by an orientation. He is affected in a number of conscious and unconscious ways by a process of specialization that began five or even seven years earlier and may even at that stage have been based on special predispositions and abilities that he already possessed. The effect is to equip him with a knowledge of special meanings (language), special preoccupations (view of the world), analytical and conceptual frameworks and ways of posing questions and directions in which to look for answers (a methodology). The power of this special approach is balanced by a weakness in the interpretation of the approaches of others. A biologist is not equipped to think and feel like an English student, or vice versa, on a whole number of issues. When graduate students leave the subject departments in which they took their first degrees, the subject sub-culture, as we have described it, takes on the form of a latent culture. That is, the special skills and agreed upon meanings are only activated in so far as the new situations in which the student finds himself make them relevant. They provide him with an array of social strategies from which he can choose. The example in this chapter of the teaching styles of French language graduates teaching English is evidence that supports the idea of latent culture. Presumably, if university graduates were scattered on leaving university and took up a random selection of occupations among others of their cohort, these latent cultures would be of little relevance in the generation of new cultures and remain in a latent state. The perspectives and sub-cultures arising in the new situations would bear little resemblance to those existing in the university. Many aspects of student sub-culture are in fact discarded in this way.

As we have seen, one of the dominating experiences of the student-teacher training year is their experience as a teacher in a classroom. This experience is almost invariably as a subject teacher, the exception is the primary group. Aspects of the subject sub-culture are revived within the context of the school and become part of an emerging subject teacher perspective. It should be clear that in examining the emerging subject teacher perspective we are looking at a *new* phenomenon. There is not a complete revival of the university subject culture, which becomes a latent culture from which skills and shared meanings are selected and put to work in new situations. These new situations transmute the old latent culture strategies and a new perspective emerges. I call this emerging perspective a 'subject teacher perspective'.

We are now in a position to view the Sussex course not as a single stranded professional induction but as a multi-stranded process in which student teachers are moving towards a profession which is itself still striving towards common understandings in vital areas of its professional practice.

The next chapter looks at student-teacher socialization within a case study. It is important to stress the limitations of the case study approach. Generalization from such a study is little more than speculation. Its strength is in the depth and detail of the analysis and the guidance it provides for those approaching other studies of professional socialization or those seeking an understanding of their own predicament.

Chapter 4

A case study: student teacher-socialization

This chapter is a chronological description of the process of becoming a teacher. It is a view obtained by participating in the activities of students both in the university and the schools in which they did their teaching practice. It is idiosyncratic. I have allowed the patterning of the chronology to develop out of my experiences. I have, however, tested it wherever I could against other data that was part of the research, but was independent of the participant observation study, for example from questionnaires.

It is implicit in the earlier chapters that the process I am describing takes place within specialized sub-cultures within the broader framework of teaching. I attempted to cover this variation by participating in the activities of two groups in any year, one on the arts side and one on the science side.

Table 4.1 *Subject groups within Sussex GEC*

1969–70					
English, French	*History*	Biology	Maths	*Physics/Chemistry*	Primary
1970–71					
English, French		*Biology*	Maths	Physics/Chemistry	Primary
1971–72					
English	History	Biology	Maths	Physics/Chemistry	Primary

The groups in which I participated in each year are in italics.

Inevitably my own preconceptions and value orientations affected the extent to which I became part of the arts group or the science group. It is, I think, fairly clear that the account that follows is richer in relation to the arts, in particular the English groups.

It is a well-known phenomena to anyone teaching in schools or universities or to anyone acquainted with research on student satisfaction that students approach a new course especially in a new college or school with high levels of enthusiasm and feelings of excitement and expectancy. It is sad but perhaps inevitable that these feelings do not last throughout the course. The slump into despondency, either with the course or ones own performance on the course, is not a simple or a continuing phenomenon. For the individual student there are enormously rewarding and enlightening experiences even when the work and strain of coping seem to be at their greatest. For the group as a whole the end of a course produces a new and special sort of attachment. They are, after all, near the point of graduating and of becoming people who are, to an extent, identified by the status conferred by the course. The status of the course is therefore something both they and their fellow 'graduates' are attached to, and this attachment produces different constraints in talking about the course or criticizing the course depending on the 'insider' or 'outsider' position of the person to whom they are talking. This was most noticeable at the end of the course at Sussex where students were encouraged to make both verbal and written criticism of the course. They frequently worried about the status of the document they had written and whether it would fall into the hands of people who did not understand the context in which the remarks were made.

This experiential cycle or spiral, since the end point differs from the beginning, was most noticeable in the context of the teacher education course at Sussex. The considerable strains of the classroom situation over the whole year seemed to produce marked extremes of euphoria, depression and exhaustion which highlighted the stages observed below.

The honeymoon period

The 'honeymoon period', as the name implies is a period of euphoria and heightened awareness. One student writing on her experiences within a comprehensive school says this explicitly:

'This introductory "honeymoon period" in a school makes us exceptionally aware of general moods which can pass unnoticed when you become an integral part of the system.'

Much of the euphoria arises from the massive change in direction in the student's career from the academic 'grind' through school and university to a practical course involving relationships with children. This seems to be true whether the student is mainly concerned with learning to teach his subject or has chosen to teach, as in the following cases, for more ideological reasons. 'We both chose to do our teaching practice at this school for, in political and human terms, we were in favour of comprehensive organization and were therefore most anxious to "live-out" the expression of such a school.' Experiences in the school are novel, students make mistakes in interpreting the inner culture of the school and are surprised and sometimes worried by what they find. The subject seminar in the first term is characteristically used as a forum to swap experiences and re-establish the more familiar stances of the university. At the end of the first week they recount how strange it sounds to be called 'Miss' or 'Sir'. How difficult it is to tell pupils apart. 'All the children look the same in the middle of the school.' While some have already had experiences that were worrying as this entry in my note book illustrates:

** Jean instanced a remark that one of her pupils had made in their written work after she had asked them to pretend they were people on the first train from Lewes to Brighton. Jean had acted as a television interviewer to the passengers as they got off the train. One child wrote 'Then some lady interviewer asked me a lot of questions. I've got no idea what they were about.'

Most students were still not sufficiently part of the school to feel worried by events that carried a warning of increasing difficulty in the future. Jean was mildly perplexed by the child's lack of understanding, yet the gulf between her own understanding of the world of school and scholarship, derived from her family, a

Note In this chapter all substantial quotations from fieldnotes are marked with a double asterisk ** in the margin. Where major sections are quoted, the date is usually given, but in any case quotations from the year 1970–71 are distinguished by the use of initials instead of names. The names of students quoted from the 1971–72 fieldnotes are disguised.

direct grant school, and Oxford, and the childrens' view, in a rural secondary modern school, was to prove a major difficulty later on.

The students were still surprised that pupils stood up when they entered the classroom and while they were prepared to admit that they did not understand why things were going well, they felt that they were. They were also optimistic about overcoming future difficulties.

The search for material and ways of teaching

The first major shift from the student to the teacher role comes through having to prepare material (notes, pictures, ideas, etc.) for the school, and in particular the classroom and its pupils, instead of for a member of the university faculty. As student teachers emerge from the 'honeymoon period' and classroom difficulties increase in their significance, the search for material becomes a more central concern. The student teacher attempts to compensate for his lack of control and lack of ability to improvise within the classroom, by elaborate preparation. The search for impressive material was recorded in a number of seminars by the third week of teaching. The end of the honeymoon and the search for material is clearly illustrated in these quotations from my fieldnotes recorded at the end of October and beginning of November. The first two quotations are from a university seminar with the English group in 1970–71.

** *1970 End of October*
   The group were concerned about discipline. M. had been impressed with Mr B. who could control a difficult class and read to them at the same time. F. had seen a teacher succeed with her group for a short time but when the noise came it was worse than ever. The work they turned in was poor; they seemed uninterested – even using modern techniques. The teacher had played the 'Pathetique' to them and asked for an imaginative essay – they had not even listened during the record ...
** I noticed that the preoccupation of the group had shifted again. The individual 'bullies', the visible problem pupil had given way to the broader problem of finding teaching material to stem the more general issue of classroom control.
   F. Suggested handouts – she had copied a Giles cartoon

which went down well – poems and parts of novels could be photocopied.

R. Suggested making up a folder of materials for the whole group to use as reserve.

F. Develop handouts that go with sets of books.

M. Use sound or film. Commentary of Clay v. Quarry fight, for example.

On these occasions the group moved closer to establishing a primitive resources bank. R's suggestion of making up a folder was elaborated in discussion to become a means of exchanging 'ideas that worked' and gave rise to good lessons. Some ideas were in fact exchanged but the ideal of close collaboration and exchange brought about by the common problem of maintaining discipline and encouraged by the E-tutor did not flourish. We shall look into the reasons for this at a later stage.

In the following year of the research a similar pattern emerged with the new cohort of students. This time it was Ned who proposed a solution.

** *1971 End of October – Beginning of November*
There was the beginning of a discussion of the sort that took place in the English group last year which I characterized as the search for material. As the students work through their first enthusiasms, they begin to search rather frantically for alternative sources. So Bob asked the question 'Where do you get your material?' Jean answered rather curtly, 'From my bookshelf.' Anne said that at present she was duplicating material from her own books.

** Everyone wanted to confess to the problems they were having in controlling the class and everyone asked anxiously about the sort of role they found themselves playing. Lisa said, 'I found myself screaming at them. I didn't want to but I had to in order to make myself heard.' All of them had emerged from the 'honeymoon period' when they had been allowed to talk to the class without interruption. They were all worried that they were behaving in the way that they didn't want to behave. At this point, Ned proposed that they examine their ideals and develop some sort of strategy for the preservation of their ideals in terms of their behaviour within the classroom. He asked why they felt they had to scream in order to make themselves heard. Surely, if we had *something interesting to say*, the kids would listen. (my italics)

Ned's solution combined the common concern about the difficulties emerging from the classroom with the growing dissatisfaction with university seminars. He proposed that the tutor stand down as leader of the seminar and that the members propose and elect a chairman. The tutor, a little bemused, but certainly not upset or discouraged agreed. Ned was then elected chairman and the seminar proceeded to discuss a programme for the rest of the term that would enable the students to examine their ideals and share the results of their experience in attempting to implement their ideals. In this seminar Ned's intervention led to a strategic redefinition of the situation but the redefinition still encapsulated and attempted to solve the problem of teaching material and ways of teaching.

In science groups the problem posed was slightly different. The material was prescribed by a packed syllabus and was abundant. The search was for a way to organize and present the material in an interesting way, despite the pressure from syllabus and examinations. The problems posed to the beginning teacher were frequently of a technical character. Science subject seminars rarely encompassed general or theoretical problems. A typical seminar might be organized around how to teach the use of the microscope.

** The microscopes we have at school are far more simple. Actually my main problem is that they are so blocked with dust and hair that you cannot see bacteria. The kids draw dust particles.

In both cases, arts and science, the student attempts to ensure the success of the lesson by detailed preparation in advance of the lesson. The search becomes less marked as students routinize, repeat and adapt a growing repertoire, learn to make a little go a long way or rely on age old answers from text books, like comprehension exercises and dictation. In addition the solutions that appear to make sense in the context of the university seem far less relevant in the context of the school. This was as true of the student-run seminar as of the more usual tutor-run seminar.

The search for material is the student-teacher's behavioural response to the problems posed by the classroom. It ties him to the classroom even though he is physically miles away from it and involves an investment of intellect and imagination that is particularly personal. It is this personal investment in the solution to

82

the problem of the classroom that makes failure or even partial failure or rejection so shattering. There can be very few professions in which professional induction involves such a high rate of initial failure by the students and rejection by the clients.

The accumulation of these experiences paves the way for the 'crisis'.

The crisis

The diagnosis of a crisis depends of course entirely on the perspective of the observer and by his criteria for judging the situation. In the situation we are examining a large number of students are at some time or another subjectively in or near a crisis situation. They feel that they are not in control of the situation, that they are failing to get through to their pupils and that they are failing to teach them. The feeling can be momentary, during a lesson, or while marking exercise books, or it can be a general state of affairs with only moments of optimism and feelings of confidence. These feelings are discussed, sometimes within the privacy of a confidential conversation and sometimes more generally within the seminar. Extracts from my fieldnotes in November 1971 illustrate the sorts of pressures the students felt and already the beginnings of protective reactions from the students are emerging.

** *November 1971*
   Bob talked of how disconcerting it was when a pupil kept coming up to him and then going away without saying anything. He thought that he was friendly and approachable enough for the pupil to unburden himself. It obviously upset him to think that the pupil thought otherwise. He talked on another occasion about seeing a boy he knew on the way home and saying 'Hello' only to see the boy change direction and walk away.

Jean's problem of communication with her rural secondary modern pupils brought her at one point to consider giving up the course.

** Jean, almost in tears and fairly incoherent, said 'I don't like the way it's going ... I'm put in situations that I don't like I sometimes feel like giving up the course!'

83

For some in the English seminar group the problems were capable of solution but in doing so developed strategies that divided the group and placed Ned's plans for the seminar under considerable tension. The following extracts from fieldwork notes contain examples of these strategies and some early analysis of the nature of the developing crisis.

** Lisa provided an example of a different sort of distancing. She had taught the top stream and had come away with the impression that they weren't very bright. She said 'My God, if they're supposed to be the top stream, goodness knows what the others in the 4th year are like.'

** The above examples (other examples similar to Lisa) show that, both from the point of view of personal relationships and from the point of view of assessment of academic potential, the students are meeting challenging situations and are both distancing and labelling in self protection. Bob had referred to the pupils he taught as 'really strange, really weird'. Lisa had referred to her 4A as 'dumb'. Lora referred to her third year boys who were trying it on and were 'really nasty'. 'You know, they have it all worked out in advance.' Anna talked about a typical challenge. She said she noticed that one boy was eating a sweet but had decided that if he did so fairly quietly she would ignore it. Presently somebody said, 'Please, Miss, David's eating a sweet. What you going to do about it?' She made him take it out, wrap it up in paper and throw it in the wastepaper bin. It was this constant challenge and having to react predictably to situations that were set up to test them that really upset the students. They felt that they didn't want to react in a sterotyped way to what seemed to them artificial situations.

The discussions reported above had two indirectly recognizable functions. The first was to communicate and share difficulties. If the problem is a general one then less blame attaches to the individual. 'We can't all be failing.' The second is to push towards a solution. If there is disorder in the classroom then the pupils can't be learning; the student therefore feels guilty. The student teacher is also on trial, his very career at stake. These are frequently unacceptable pressures and the student begins to push the blame for these failures away from himself. There are two recognizable directions in which this blame can go: 1. Upwards towards the 'system', the head, the other teachers, that is the radical direction. 2. Downwards towards the pupils, that is the establishment response. Most student teachers fluctuated in pushing sometimes in one direction and sometimes in the other. However, within the discussion in the seminars some took firm stands and a recognizable polarity developed. In the quotations already reported, Jean blames the system: 'I'm put in situations I don't like', while Lisa and Lora were already beginning to blame the pupils. Lisa, for example, states, 'My God, if they're supposed to be the top stream ...' and Lora refers to the third year boys as 'really nasty'.

The following description of part of a seminar in November 1971 illustrates in greater detail the way problems encountered in the classroom are displaced either by 'blaming' the system or accepting the system and 'blaming' the child. Classroom strategies are advocated that are in line with these differing and developing perspectives. It also illustrates the growing dissension within the student led seminar which eventually prevented it from moving towards the goals they had set themselves.

** Lisa observed that her non-exam forms weren't interested. 'Maybe it was a mistake to drop English literature exams.'

Ned questioned her on this: 'Exams are good for whom? Don't you mean good for you? It enables you to impose on the kids what you want.'

Lisa: 'The school expects me to be a policeman and you are a failure if you are not. You will have to play the role.'

Ned: 'No, that's just want I don't want to do. You should bring yourself to the situation and allow them (the pupils) to bring their problems and you to bring your problems.'

The discussion broadened as people recounted the difficulties involved in allowing pupils to have 'free' expression. Jean, Bob, and Ned continued to advocate it.

Lora found that an imaginative exercise on advertising that she thought would go well was a flop. The class preferred a routine comprehension lesson that would prepare them for an exam.

This led Lisa back to her attack on Ned.

Lisa: 'They don't read books unless they have the stimulus of an exam.'

Bob: 'Then why don't you let them read in the lesson?'

Ned came back to his attack on Lisa, accusing her of wanting an easy life and making use of exams. He didn't agree with 'O' or 'A' levels.

Lisa: 'You have a responsibility to the children and therefore you must accept society as it is.'

Ned complained that the only time the teacher was free to experiment outside the exam system was in the remedial streams when the kids were already destroyed by the system.

The link between the direction of displacement of 'blame' and a radical-conservative dimension is I think fairly clear. The displacement of 'blame' is a central part of the next process I wish to discuss, which can be characterized as 'learning to get by'.

Learning to get by (and failure)

I have reported that a fairly high but unspecified proportion of students feel themselves to be in a crisis or near crisis situation at some time during the early part of their teaching practice. During this period the student feels the need to communicate about his problems and displaces the 'blame'. There are, however, limits to the extent a student is able to do this without damaging his standing as prospective teacher, that is, without damaging the assumption that he will 'get by' and make a good teacher in the end.

There are a number of strategies a student-teacher may adopt in dealing with the problems of the teaching situation. It is possible to suggest two major categories under which most of the observed strategies are subsumed. The first category involves a *'collectivization'* of the problem. The problem is shared by the group whose collective opinions legitimize the displacement of blame. The second category involves the *'privatization'* of the problem. The student doesn't speak about it, except in a most guarded way, and may refuse to admit to any problem at all, in certain situations. Once again some students remain true to one or other of these basic strategies throughout the course, many shift from one to another, depending on the situational constraints. Most of these shifts are moderate, within the middle ground, but on occasion dramatic shifts take place over the extreme range. These dramatic shifts characteristically occur when a student is defined as 'at risk' or failing to get by. It is within this sometimes abruptly changed situation, that students re-define friends and enemies and 'collectivize' or 'privatize' their problems accordingly.

It is perhaps important to notice that the extent to which a subject group will legitimize the displacement of blame depends to some extent on agreement about the direction of displacement (i.e., the radical or establishment direction). Within the subject groups I observed, sub-groups and even cliques sometimes formed around this issue. On some occasions after basic disagreements had been aired the solidarity of the group was reaffirmed by discussing a topic like the unsatisfactory way students were treated by schools. It was nearly always possible to get a group cohering in a radical direction on this topic, for example:

** *Late November 1971*

Anna complained that she wasn't allowed to go to the stock cupboard on her own and that she couldn't select a 4th year play for a 3rd year class. Michael complained that the largest area of derogatory treatment came from cooks and secretaries. Lisa said that at her school the cooks had separated the students and staff and when she sat in the wrong place, one of the cooks immediately ordered her out of it and said 'How are we expected to know the difference between staff and students if you sit in the wrong place?' Brenda complained . . .

The result of sessions like the above was that the students all felt closer together and able to plan collective action for example future seminars. It is important to note, however, that the accord had been obtained by discussing the problems of their own student-teacher status in school and not in the area of teacher-pupil relationships which had been the initial aim of the student-run group.

In discussing the stresses that affect the position of the student-teacher I have now introduced four *observed* types of social strategy, 'collectivizing' and 'privatizing' strategies, upward and downward displacement of blame, which are emerging perspectives within the teacher role. It is now important that we examine the implications of these strategies for 'learning to get by' or 'failure' within the course. In addition we should remember the three *theoretical* types of strategy: strategic compliance, internalized adjustment and strategic redefinition.

Although the Sussex course has no formal examination and no gradation of success (merit, distinction etc.), the 'fail' category remains. In the absence of formal examinations much of the responsibility for assessing the pass-fail outcome for each student rests with his teacher-tutor. The Sussex student who feels near crisis is therefore in a bind. If he unburdens himself to the man who is in many respects most able to help, he risks revealing the true depth of his difficulties and by his own admission demonstrates that he is unable to get by. For many teacher-tutors this can be overcome by making a close affective relationship with their student and jettisoning the assessor role. But for those who attempt both a close relationship and an assessor role the dilemma is deepened. The close relationship with the student, if successful, releases the student from his bind and he openly confesses to his difficulties and perhaps even to a radical direction in his displacement of blame. If the student's difficulties continue the tutor reaches the point where he feels he has a duty to report these difficulties and the student is 'at risk'. He may be prompted in this by the feeling that not only has this student got difficulties, but that the direction in which he is looking for a solution is unlikely to provide him with one. From the student's perspective this reversal of his tutor's role seems like a betrayal. His tutor has shifted from mentor to inquisitor and the very openness of the relationship at the early stages seems in retrospect a trap. This feeling may lead to a change in the relationship between student and tutor and to a further deterioration in the student's position within the school. In these circumstances, the teacher-tutor may ask for the student to be failed.

The extreme development of these factors as described above occurred only two or three times in the 3 years of the study. However, the extreme development of factors in unusual cases can be used to highlight constraints that underlie the more normal relationship but remain hidden. In normal circumstances they are dealt with successfully by the behavioural strategies of the actors.

There is one more point to be made about cases at risk before we turn to their more general importance. The configuration of factors in these cases brings about a maximum divergence between the E-tutor (or university tutors) and the teacher-tutor. The openness of the student in collectivizing his problem may have made him a valuable member of the university seminars, with a reputation for frankness and sensitivity. The student is not therefore without allies in the debate about failure.

In the cases mentioned above there was a combination of social strategies that produced a particularly vulnerable position for the student-teacher.

Table 4.2

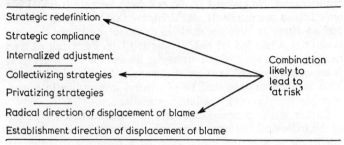

The success of the student who combines these strategies depends to a large extent on the success of his ability to redefine the situation. In one case a student who we shall call Peter was reported in the first term as having a serious and conscientious attitude towards teaching; preparing his work with great thoroughness; being pleasant in manner and helpful and having little difficulty with discipline. He became the opposite on all those counts before the end of the third term. By this time, according to the school, he had become weak in class control, failed to prepare lessons, showed lack of responsibility to the school and thought the responsible tutors at the school were 'getting at him'. Associated with this reassessment, although not necessarily accounting for it, was a long open debate about such issues as deschooling, group work, work sheets, integrated teaching, and mixed ability teaching, in which Peter had advocated radical change. On most of these issues Peter had differed from his tutor and, even more importantly, had failed to employ compliance strategies at crucial points during the process of moving to an 'at risk' classification. He had certainly not appreciated the extent to which he had failed to redefine the situation and when he found himself 'at risk' was deeply hurt and upset; he felt he was being victimized.

A possible mechanism of socialization is revealed by this analysis. If 'radical' students who use collectivizing strategies in school fail to carry off their performance within the classroom or the staffroom they must sensitively adjust to a compliance strategy. In the case under discussion, the student had taught successfully using conventional methods even in the summer term. According to the school it was his lack of ability when using innovatory methods and his insistence on using them that put him at risk. The student also felt sure that if he had carried on in the traditional manner he would have satisfied the tutor's requirements. He claimed he did not do so because it would not have helped the pupils. It would appear that the normal signals and adjustments were not made in this case and by the time the student was labelled 'at risk' it was too late. Peter felt obliged to fight on the basis of the strategies he was currently using. It is important to note the effect of the at risk labelling in this case. This mechanism may well be of general importance in understanding the effects of labelling in socialization.

Earlier in the previous chapter I emphasized that the ability of the individual to carry out a particular strategy was an important factor in selecting it and creating a place for it within an institution. In the present case we have seen that Peter was unable to create a place for his teaching strategies within the school. His was an attempt at strategic redefinition of a situation that failed. However, an additional mechanism was at work. Peter had not appreciated how badly he was failing to redefine the situation and to what extent his attempts at innovation within the classroom were unacceptable to his tutor. This sensitivity to the environment and to significant others within it, was a dimension of individual behaviour picked up in a study of undergraduates at Edinburgh University conducted by Carolyn Miller and Malcolm Parlett (1974). I have quoted their report *Up to the Mark* at some length because the research, undertaken at about the same time as the tutorial schools research, throws additional light on the issue of sensitivity to situations.

'Cues' and the consciousness students have of them

When we started interviewing final year honours students in one of the departments studied, we were not concentrating particularly on *individual* differences in students' approaches to assessment: indeed, we were concerned more with what was common or shared. However, when we began the detailed analysis of the data at the end of all the interviews, individual differences began to show up strongly and could not be ignored. The chief distinguishing features were as follows. One group of students talked about a need to be perceptive and receptive to 'cues' sent out by staff – things like picking up hints about exam topics, noticing which aspects of the subject the staff favoured, noticing whether they were making a good impression in a tutorial and so on. These students seemed to believe that these factors were terribly important in what their final degree marks would be based on.

There was another, smaller group of students who were further distinguished in having, over and above this receptiveness of perceptiveness towards cues, an *activity* component. Unlike the first group, they were not just content to pick up hints and to wonder if they were making a good impression. Instead they deliberately interacted with the system: they button-holed staff about the exam questions; sought them out over coffee; made a point of discovering who their oral examiner was, what his interests were, and most of all, deliberately attempted to make a good impression on staff. This for them seemed to constitute a very large part of what the exams were all about. We have called these people, who are characterized by their dynamic interacting way of behaving, '*cue-seekers*'. The first group, who were perceptive without the activity component, we have called '*cue-conscious*'.

The third group, and the largest, had neither perceptive nor active components – and we labelled them, perhaps rather unkindly, '*cue-deaf*'. For them, it seemed that working as hard as you could was the ingredient for success. They believed that the impression they made on staff – if they did make one – would not affect the way in which they were marked. Nor did they speak of picking up hints.

The differences between students in what we decided to term their 'cue-consciousness', was something that we had not predicted and which emerged from analysis after the interviews. We should emphasize here that the three types (cue-seekers, cue-conscious and cue-deaf) are shorthand, descriptive terms and not to be taken as rigid categories or as formally defined psychological types. Theoretically, a category system here, rather than a continuum, is somewhat artificial. Given that we found these three major types, that is not to say that there are not finer gradations between them. However, elaboration of these would necessarily depend on a more focused study than was warranted here. Cue-consciousness is a concept that extends previous ideas of the hidden curriculum in a useful way.

We must remember that this description and analysis relates to a different situation in which undergraduates are competing for a degree classification. There is therefore no reason to suppose that cue-seeking will be as prominent an activity within a PGCE course. On the other hand the analysis illustrates the way that students under considerable stress from examinations can exploit their sensitivity to the informal structure or as Snyder (1971) has called it, 'the hidden curriculum', to obtain better grades. Peter made the mistake of allowing his cue-consciousness within the university setting to stand instead of cue-consciousness within the school. He ignored the cues from the school until it was too late. Peter became 'cue-deaf' within the school because of a commitment to an alternative way of teaching and relating to pupils. Although Peter was put 'at risk' he eventually passed the course with support from university staff.

For the average student, the bind described above is most frequently resolved by adapting strategies that differentiate between the school and university. We have seen that the strategies typical of the university are collectivist while those employed within the school tend to be privatized. Very little questionnaire evidence was collected on this issue but the evidence presented below bears obliquely on it. Combined with the other evidence it amounts to, I believe, a strong case.

The rough classification of student strategies that follows comes from the questionnaire item that asked the students to report on differences between E-tutors and teacher-tutors and how they coped with the differences. It is important to notice that the descriptions involve a high degree of student-teacher autonomy and choice, an active engagement and interpretation rather than internationalized adjustment. Most of the strategies illustrated in the table below would be classified as strategic compliance or strategic redefinition. For example, number 4 clearly represents strategic compliance and the rather plaintive note struck in number 5 summarizes a long history of debate and dispute which come close to the failed strategic redefinition strategy described earlier. The strategies reported are nearly all examples of privatized strategies. It is noticeable that the teacher-tutor is more frequently the subject of these strategies than the E-tutor. In this, the classification accurately represents the total data and illustrates the point made above that privatized strategies are more likely to be related to school.

Strategies ignoring teacher-tutor

1 The role of English in the curriculum – I coped with it by ignoring my teacher-tutor.

2 Often it wasn't worth bringing conflict with teacher-tutor to a head, since there was a definite non-communication and it was a waste of precious school time. It was more useful and peaceful to go away and do your own thing quietly.

Strategies deceiving teacher-tutor

3 Evasion.

4 Although I disagreed with my teacher-tutor, the only way to cope was to concur with her when she was present, i.e. discipline of children/approach to timetable/art work/importance of art and the story in the curriculum.

Student differing from both

5 On most things, they were different and I was different from them both. It's too long to explain.

6 The teacher-tutor was at all times more recognizant of the concrete teaching situation, whereas the E-tutor preferred to talk in theoretical terms. I balanced the two viewpoints by recognizing the constraints which governed their thinking.

Student ignoring E-tutor in practice

7 The teacher-tutor was, of necessity, more in favour of audio-visual methods than the E-tutor. This simply meant that in practical terms one used those aspects of the method in class which produced the best response and discussed the philosophical impossibility of the entire exercise with E-tutor.

8 Introduction of Nuffield 'A' level biology syllabus. E-tutor favoured. Teacher-tutor qualified enthusiasm, favoured gradual incorporation of some curriculum material but not change of exam syllabus. I agreed with E-tutor in principle and with teacher-tutor in practice.

The classification pivots about strategies five and six, in which the student differs from both E-tutor and the teacher-tutor. The extreme strategies three and four, deceiving the tutor, are only reported as occurring with respect to the teacher-tutor role.

The data presented in the above analysis contrasts the school and the university. Further evidence of the tension between school and university culture came from participant observation. We have already seen the way Ned was able to redefine the subject seminar within the university so that student teachers could make clear their ideals and aims and make sure that these were

93

in line with their teaching strategies in school. This reorganization of the seminar was an activity of a kind unheard of within the school. On the other hand the idea that groups within the course should act in this way was not new. Other groups had, with encouragement, expressed varying degrees of autonomy. The very design of the team within the school of two students and a teacher-tutor, backed up by an E-tutor within the university had been intended by the university designers of the course to make possible this sort of collective activity within the school.

The almost complete failure of the Sussex scheme to generally involve students and teacher-tutors in a collective teaching experience within the classroom was demonstrated by our research. We can see that this failure sprung from the factors described in this analysis and from the privatized nature of the school culture. Very few students even bothered to report that they did not attempt this exercise within the school. An exercise that seemed so obviously beneficial from the vantage point of the university was almost automatically discarded once within the school. One student who did report the difficulty is reported in the following extract:

** *October 1971*

Mike was worried about the policy of teaching as a team. He thought that it was 'a physical impossibility'. He said that he would be quite willing to try it after he had settled down but the idea of making a lot of mistakes with someone else in the room he would find upsetting. His partner at the school agreed with this and was just as anxious to avoid the situation as he was. The E-tutor was sympathetic but said that so much was to be gained from seeing one's partner make mistakes and sharing mistakes that it was a pity that they should not make more of the opportunity and added 'I quite understand that you don't want someone around when that steely edge comes into your voice'.

The privatizing effect of the problems emerging from the classroom and that 'steely edge' in the voice were a marked feature of the participant observation data relating to the school, in contrast to the university.

In the following quotation, the student was surprised and a little horrified by the transformation of his fellow student as that

94

steely edge came into her voice. He was carrying some heavy recording equipment for her.

** *December 1970*
    M. I went with her to the classroom, she put some books down
    on the table and turned towards me. She had already changed
    – her lips were tight and her face had tensed and changed
    completely. She said 'put it down over there' – just like that.
    It was too late to say anything so I got out quick.

Teaching strategies devised within the collectivizing atmosphere of the university were simply dropped when the student experienced the 'realities' of the school. 'I agreed with the E-tutors in principle and with the teacher-tutor in practice.'

Learning to get by for many Sussex students therefore contains a large element of strategic compliance. The tension between the school and the university cannot easily be resolved by internalized adjustment because adjustments made in one milieu are challenged by the need to make new adjustments in a second milieu within the same week.

Conclusion

The methodology used in the research described in this chapter is close to the anthropological tradition within sociology. It attempts to build up a conceptual structure that describes the major elements of the process of professional socialization as these elements came to the notice of the researcher who was closely immersed within that process. The last two chapters of the book have viewed this process in complementary ways. Chapter 3 uses the concept of latent culture and describes the influence of subject sub-cultures on the emerging subject teacher perspectives of the students. Chapter 4 uses a developmental scheme to describe some of the common experiences of students as they take up a teacher perspective. Running through both sections of the chapter is a concern with the concept of social strategy and the implication that the individual actor, who is at the intersection of 'biography' and the 'social situation' has some freedom to manipulate and change the situation while at the same time being constrained to adjust to it.

Chapter 5

In the previous chapter a model of socialization was developed which can be described by the phrase; socialization as the adoption or creation of appropriate social strategies. The various components of the model have emerged through the discussion of five case studies of student-teacher socialization; in particular the Sussex Case Study.

The major theoretical characteristics of a number of models of socialization were discussed in Chapter 1. I raised the issue of the way functionalist models assumed internalization of social norms and high degrees of institutional stability. The model I have proposed makes the issue of internalization problematic. Within this model the actor has a choice with respect to his relationship to the social strategy he employs. He can internalize all the supporting arguments and values – internalized adjustment – or he can 'get by' and remain only partially convinced by them – strategic compliance. Beyond this, he can attempt to wrestle with the constraints of the situation and in a sense hold the institution at bay – strategic redefinition. Most strategies of this sort are highly dependent on the skill and commitment of the individual and persistent failure to redefine the situation from a position of weakness, like that of the student or beginning teacher can lead to serious problems in qualifying. In addition it must be remembered that the change produced by a successful strategic redefinition of the situation will not necessarily be permanent. For example, when Ned left at the end of his course, the original structure of the university seminar reasserted itself in the following year and the tutor once more ran the seminar. Why, if strategic redefinition is rare, its implementation dangerous and its effects often local and short lived, should we be concerned with it as a possibility? The answer lies in the importance of understanding social change and in what I have described as the sociology of the possible. Social change often proceeds in an unpredictable and apparently erratic manner. Institutional practices that have remained unchanged for many years and have been the subject of many abortive attempts at strategic redefinition suddenly change and the issues that were fought over on a number of occasions, very soon become irrelevancies. Schools and universities provide many good examples of such change.

When I was carrying out research in grammar schools in 1963, it was a common sight to see pupils lined up outside the headmaster's study to receive judgement on the length of their hair. Those whose hair was thought to be too long were given twenty-four hours to get it cut or were caned. A few years after this, one could see masters in the same school wearing their hair at a length that would have earned their pupils a caning in 1963. In the same way internal organization of a school or university, has in my experience often changed quite abruptly and all the hard fought issues about express streams, or mixed-ability groups have disappeared within months.

Examples of this type of abrupt change followed by an acceptance of the change and an apparent death of the issue are not restricted to schools. As a young lecturer I once fought a bitter struggle to obtain acceptance for a student to take my course and be examined by dissertation instead of a three hour unseen examination. In committee serious problems were predicted and it was only after a hard fought battle that permission was obtained. A few years later when I revisited the University I asked a new lecturer about the examining procedures and he estimated that something like a third of the students on some courses took the dissertation option. When I asked whether this posed a problem with some of his colleagues he replied that as far as he knew the University had always practised the dissertation option quite freely. The 'innovation' was in fact less than five years old.

It is easy within the time scale in which most of us live our everyday lives to forget the potency of social change. The historical changes illustrated in the quotations below from Ian McEvans (1976) article reminds us of the time scale of a number of radical changes. The period is, after all, only twice the life span of the average woman. If we assume that the rate of social change has doubled over this period we can expect that the average individual will see social change of this dimension, *within* his or her lifetime.

> It was not easy in the England of the late 1820's to set up a zoo, animals were not a very serious consideration. When a bill was put before Parliament proposing to protect horses and donkeys from savage usage the house dissolved into fall-about laughter, and the Lords, with a little more equanimity, dismissed the bill as undignified material for legislation. Similarly zoology was thought of as a rather silly, eccentric concern ... as Charles Kingsley was to write much later, ... the naturalist was regarded as a 'milk sop who went bug-hunting because he had not the spirit to follow the fox'.... Charles Darwin's *Origin of the Species* was not published until 1859 ... The orthodox view held by all good Christians was that the world and everything to be found in it began around 4,000 B.C. with Creation. Bull baiting was only just losing its position as the nation's favourite sport. Cock fighting was indulged in by the very fashionable led by the King himself – the First Gentleman.
>
> It was one of those times when the gap between the public attitude and the attitudes of serious thinkers could not be bridged instantly.

If we simply assume that present attitudes on conservation and ecology held by 'serious thinkers' will become widely accepted and embedded in established institutions within the next seventy years the change in our environment will be considerable. The exercise also predicts that emerging academic disciplines, no more than tolerated at the present time, could be making a major contribution to the understanding of our lives within one life span.

The rapidity of social change in the circumstances described in the first two examples is consistent with the notion of strategic compliance. It would be very difficult using orthodox sociological techniques and functionalist sociological theory to differentiate between an institution, for example, a school in which a majority of the teachers were employing internalized adjustment strategies, and one in which a majority were employing strategic compliance strategies. It would be unusual for the orthodox sociologist to pursue the individual teacher's idea of the purpose of certain of his actions and the context in which that purpose is a relevant one. Yet quite clearly the implications for social change could be very different. If a majority of teachers were strategically complying with the school's established practice of streaming and teaching a highly differentiated curriculum the result of an attempt to de-stream might be far more rapid and far reaching than in a school where this was not the case. And yet because the school is often a privatized culture the strategic nature of the compliance might be unknown right up to the time of the decision. The sociology of the possible enjoins the sociologist to enter much more openly into a mutual examination of his findings with the teachers in the situations he has studied. It is through this second level of analysis that the researcher tests the possibilities of alternative action implied in his first analysis.

For example, when carrying out my study of Hightown Grammar I thought it important to inform the headmaster of major developments within the study. As my analysis of the streaming system developed I kept him informed. During the study a new headmaster was appointed and he decided to de-stream. While the decision had not been taken as a result of my research, the research certainly influenced it. Unfortunately my research stance had been developed on the assumption that I was researching a stable situation. My first priority was therefore to salvage what I could from the situation and proceed with my analysis of the streamed section of the school. My analysis of the de-streamed structure and its effects came second. The stance I am advocating as the sociology of the possible would have enabled me to exploit the changing situation in a positive way. It was clear that a small number of senior staff had gone along with the previous policy of streaming but their attachment was one of strategic compliance. Thus their 'socialization' into the organizational structure and goals of the school as seen by the previous head had never been more than partial.

The understanding of socialization and social change is clearly closely linked. Up to this point we have been concerned to examine the link between the individual and the institution as expressed by the social strategies adopted by the individual. It is also important to consider the nature of the latent culture skills and values brought by the individual to the institution. Our analysis of Peter's crisis and Ned's redefinition of the seminar in chapter 4 makes it clear that these skills and values will affect the strategies adopted by the individual.

The following diagram demonstrates one way in which the relationship between skills and values brought to the institution (school) constrain the strategies employed within it.

Table 5.1

Nature of skills and values brought by an individual, in relation to those predicated by the institution. (school)	Strategies likely to be adopted		
	Strategic Redefinition	Strategic Compliance	Internalized Adjustment
A Skills: limited to or in excess of those necessary for the job Values: coincide with institution	1. ←-----------	2. --------------	3. -----X
B Skills: limited to those necessary for the job Values: differ from institution	4.	5. X----	6. ----→
C Skills: in excess of those necessary for the job Values: differ from institution	7. X----	8. ----→	9.

X marks the preferred social strategy for categories A, B and C.

⟶ Shows the strategy to which the individual would move if his/her skill were not sufficient to maintain the preferred strategy.

----→ Shows the possible movement of an individual whose level of skill, indeed virtuosity produces an innovation out of line with the norms and values of himself and the institution.

The above scheme describes the nature of the link between the individual and the institution and the latent culture, skills and values brought by the individual. It is important to differentiate between skills and values because in many circumstances institutional practices are adopted by an individual simply because he or she has no option. There is no alternative way of carrying out the task that will actually work for *that* individual. We have seen that this is particularly true for some student-teachers, for example, Peter the mathematics student-teacher. The scheme is not intended to describe the complexity of the issues that concern the individual in his relationship with an institution. An individual can have values that coincide with the institution in some respects and not others, and have skills that enable him to experiment with some areas of his work and not others.

In this classification and summary I have taken the institution as given. This is an over-simplification. Individuals are able to choose institutions or parts of institutions in which to work or train. In selecting a training institution it might well be the aim of individuals to find a college or department of education relevant to the skills and the values he or she holds i.e. an innovatory institution or an institution with a reputation for perfecting traditional skills.

In this chapter we will examine some of the data from the questionnaire study to see if we can find evidence of this selection on the part of the students. How far are they able to effect the nature of the institution and the course it offers by making choices, by voting with their feet.

We have already examined data which gives an indication that some selective mechanism may be at work. For example we saw that the recruitment of students to university departments of education and colleges of education gives rise to distinct patterns. In other words the composition of the student body is affected by constraining and determining forces. Traditionally these constraining factors have been given great emphasis in sociological interpretation. It is clear that some factors have a direct constraining influence for example, failure to obtain sufficiently high 'A' level qualifications will directly determine whether a student can take a degree or a college certificate but others are open to student choice. The existence of an innovatory course structure will therefore attract some students and repel others. The interplay of choice and constraint is an issue we will now examine using data from the Tutorial Schools Research Project (1973). Let us look first at the reasons given by *students* for selecting a particular course.

Reasons for selecting the university

All students were asked their opinion on the importance of a series of factors influencing their choice of university. The students were asked to respond in two ways, first by scoring all the items using a three point scale and secondly by choosing which they considered to be the *most* important factor in determining their choice of university. The data presented here refers only to the second response, but both sets of data display the same pattern.

Table 5.2 *Most important factor influencing choice of university*

	Sussex %	York %	Brunel %	Southampton %	Kings %
1. Content of course	11	50	36	17	9
2. Organization of teaching practice	46	4	6	2	6
3. Reputation of university	7	15	9	6	15
4. Familiarity with university	5	4	0	16	8
5. Desire for change	3	8	3	9	11
6. Geographical setting	8	11	25	16	18
7. Personal reasons	20	8	21	34	34
	100	100	100	100	101
n =	62	74	33	196	105

Source: TSRP (1973)

The factors in the table are arranged to constitute a progression. The first two factors refer to the internal arrangements of the course itself, the next three factors refer to the university and the final two refer to factors external to both the course and the university. The differences between the universities are in detail fairly complex and in most cases reflect accurately the differences in emphasis of the university courses. For example, Sussex is chosen predominantly because of the way it organizes its teaching practice whereas York and Brunel are chosen because of the content of their courses.

In order to simplify the table for the purposes of comparison we can make use of the arrangement of the factors described above.

Table 5.3 *Most important factor influencing choice of university – simplified*

	Sussex %	York %	Brunel %	Southampton %	Kings %
Factors concerning the course	57	54	42	19	15
Factors outside course and university (geographical and personal)	28	19	45	50	52

Source: TSRP (1973)

In this simplified table the broad pattern is immediately apparent. The new universities recruit students who see themselves as being attracted in the main by the content and organization of the course that is offered while students at the old universities see themselves as being attracted, in the main, by factors outside the consideration of course and university. For example, 'chance to spend one year more in London, after being away some time'; 'loyalty to home church'; 'accessible to mother and friends'; 'remaining in circle of university friends'; 'to be within easy reach of my fiancée' are a sample of the 'most important' reasons given for choosing the older universities. It is important not to generalize from the rather specific meaning of this evidence. It would not be safe, for example, to infer that Sussex or York students were therefore more committed to teaching or even to the university of their choice than the students of the old universities. We are looking at the reasons students give for having made a certain choice. What we have seen is that students see themselves as motivated by different considerations in making these choices.

The process of recruiting students into departments of education varies enormously in its organization between universities. Some undertake to interview all possible candidates, others interview only a few. Some subject groups in some universities are vastly oversubscribed in terms of applications, giving the university staff a large measure of choice in making up their groups. Other subjects, sometimes within the same university, are hard pushed to make up their numbers and accept practically anyone who applies, chemistry and maths, for example. We did not collect data on the details of these recruitment procedures. In general, however, two selection processes can be seen to be at work.

First, the student selects the university departments of his choice and, secondly, the university staff chooses the student from among the group thus made available. The process is therefore one of select and be selected. We are in no position to allocate relative strengths to these processes in determining the character of the groups that are finally recruited. However, one member of the team participated very fully in the selection process at Sussex for two consecutive years and was able to record that students who understood and were enthusiastic about the particular nature of the Sussex course were more likely to be chosen than those who were not and who were likely to be seen as 'out of touch with' the major objectives of the course. It would seem likely, therefore, that in the main, both the 'select' and 'be selected' parts of the recruitment process work in the same direction to produce groups of students who reflect in the characteristics they possess some of the characteristics of the university departments to which they are recruited.

In comparing the characteristics of the newly recruited student bodies, we are therefore saying something about the character of the departments concerned. It must be made clear that we are not implying that the characteristics that we present are necessarily the same as those used in the selection process. We are not, for example, suggesting that because Kings is highest on the 'education' and 'social background of parents' indices that this is in itself a criterion used by the staff for recruiting students.

The fact that students exercise some control over the choice of university means that they do influence an important aspect of the course itself. They ensure that a higher proportion of their colleagues will share similar ideas about the course and about education. This mechanism is also one that influences the recruitment of staff of schools, for example the early comprehensive schools and the early open-plan schools attracted staff in sympathy with these developments. It has not been widely exploited in the recruitment of school staff in general.

A second method of examining the way students felt about their courses was to ask specifically about the major structural components of their courses. In this question the major structural components of the Sussex course were opposed to their counterparts in the traditional course. The students were required to mark on a seven point scale how much they approved of each component by marking the scale nearest to the option they most approved, for example:

Teaching practice arranged   Teaching practice
throughout the year ...... 7 6 5 4 3 2 1 ...... in discrete blocks.

In the table below each university is scored according to how
much its students approved of its *own* option. It must be remembered however, that each student was presented with the same
choice in the questionnaire.

Table 5.4 *Mean score made by student-teachers in favour of the elements of
their own courses. Beginning of course Autumn 1970*

	Sussex	York	Brunel	Southampton	Kings
TP throughout year versus discrete blocks	6·61	5·26	5·15	5·39	5·25
Supervision. University tutor versus tutor from school staff	5·75	4·14	3·93*	4·28	4·42
TP in one school versus two or more schools	4·34	4·77	4·11	5·11	3·80*
Less than ½ course in school versus more than ½ in school	5·48	5·44	4·52	5·31	3·67*
TP split week versus 5 days/week	6·29	5·33	5·70	5·62	4·74
Mean score	5·69	4·99	4·68	5·14	4·37

N.B. A score of 4 indicates the mid point between options.
* Scores marked thus are marginally in favour of the Sussex structure
  on this item.
Source: TSRP (1973)

The scores show clearly that Sussex students are more in favour
of their course structure than the students at any of the other
universities. In fact there is only one item (Teaching practice in one
school versus more than one school) where any other university
surpasses Sussex. It is important to point out that Sussex students
did not score as high on detailed questions about the *content* of
the course. On this issue students from other universities were
without exception more in favour of their courses than Sussex
students. Thus in a situation where students are conscious of

105

choosing a course which has an innovatory *structure* they are also in favour of the specific elements of the structure to a greater degree than students of other courses. This finding must add significance to the earlier table.

If we now assume that choice of institution is part of a student's array of legitimate strategies for controlling some aspects of the institutional environment in which he will learn or work we can proceed in a speculative but grounded way to illustrate the two processes that interest us within professional socialization. We have already identified these processes within a single course through a predominantly participant observation methodology. Now we can view the broad spectrum of five university departments and use a comparative approach. The two processes are, on the one hand those that affect all students and evoke a response with important common elements, like the 'honeymoon period', and on the other hand those that give rise to a differentiated response like cue-consciousness.

Of course most phenomena enable both mechanisms to occur simultaneously, so that in looking at the emerging subject teacher perspective we were able to recognize it as a perspective involving many common elements but at the same time differentiated by latent and reconstituted subject sub-culture elements.

The remaining part of this chapter is divided into two sub-sections; the first examines data which illustrates the common elements in the process; the second examines some characteristics which appear to differentiate the students within the overall picture. In this second sub-section an attempt is made to characterize one differentiating process which seems to be important in shaping our teachers and our schools.

Let us continue by examining the data on how students' perceptions of their reasons for teaching changed during the training year, and examine some of the broad and general changes that take place as the students move through their training year. Even at this stage, however, it will be possible to point out some variation between universities.

An examination of some of the common elements within the process of student-teacher socialization

A large number of items were presented to the students on this topic and respondents were invited to score each item using a scale 1–5 with 5 representing 'very important' and 1 'not at all

106

important'. The results of the initial response are presented below. The responses were ranked for each university in terms of the mean scores and a final ranking arrived at by calculating the mean rank for each item.

Table 5.5 *Student-teacher perceptions of their reasons for teaching – 1970*

Overall rank of Question	Items (abbreviated)	Mean rank for 5 universities
1.	Like seeing progress made by children as they become aware of things	1·4
2.	Enjoy doing something creative	2·6
3.	Like using talents to full	3·4
4.	Challenge of changing situation	4·0
5.	Like teaching own subject	4·6
6.	Like keeping up with subject	5·8
7.	Like gaining child's confidence	6·6
8.	Preparing them to build new society	8·4
9.	Guide towards suitable career	9·8
10.	Want to increase self-knowledge	11·0
	Children help you keep open mind	11·0
12.	Can be fitted around other commitments	11·4
13.	Pursue own hobbies in holidays	12·2
14.	Possibilities for advancement	12·4
15.	Like being able to rest in holidays	15·4
16.	Influence next generation	16·4
17.	Like to feel will always have steady income	16·8
18.	Change young people's attitudes	17·4
19.	Little danger of being out of job	18·8
20.	Companionship of staffroom	19·8

Source: TSRP (1973)

There is a very clear attachment to 'idealistic' reasons for taking up teaching. The top four reasons combine an interest in the progress made by children, enjoyment in doing something creative, using one's talents to the full and accepting the challenge of a changing situation. In contrast the bottom four reasons contain three which deal with conditions of the job, a steady income, job security and the companionship of the staffroom. The similarity between universities in this general pattern is most marked.

After a year of training which in each university included teaching practice in schools, an interesting and again surprisingly similar pattern of change occurred. These changes are recorded in the following table. Each item is scored for each university and given a '+' if it gained in perceived importance as a reason for teaching and the gain or loss is indicated in a rough way by the recording of levels of significance. These levels should be interpreted as follows:

(n.s.)   Small gain or loss, not statistically significant
(10%)
(5%)   Gains or losses of increasing statistical significance
(2%)   i.e. larger.
(1%)
(0.1%)

There are marked increases in items relating to job security, holidays and income, and large significant decreases in items relating to doing something creative, the challenge of the situation and using one's talents to the full.

We will accumulate a number of these findings before proceeding with an analysis.

In 1970 students were asked how important they felt various experiences should be in the teacher training year. The result showed a clear pattern of expectation extending across all universities. Students came to their courses with well developed notions of the relative importance of expected experiences. The PGCE would be a practical course in which they must learn to *teach* their *subject*. They needed fitting out with the latest teaching methods and knowledge of the running of a school. In this process they would need to be helped by a knowledge of psychology, sociology and self knowledge. Theories of education and philosophy were of less importance, so was knowledge of individual children. Very few considered any *further* knowledge of their subject to be necessary and educational administration was also of slight importance. Table 5.7 shows the initial rank order of these items averaged for the five universities.

The overall pattern of change is also clear. After experiencing their course, including the teaching practice with its exposure to the classroom situation, their reassessment of the elements of the course is striking. The three theoretical aspects of the course, psychology, sociology and philosophy all decline in importance. They apparently fail to achieve their promise; they do not assist in the practical job of becoming a teacher in anything like the degree that was expected. On the other hand the practical aspects

Table 5.6 Change in student-teacher perceptions of their 'reasons for teaching' recorded for the total duration of the course

Description of Orientation	Reasons for Teaching (abbreviated)	Initial Rank	University				
			Sussex	York	Brunel	Southampton	Kings
Subject	Like teach own subject	5	− (ns)	− (ns)	− (ns)	− (ns)	− (ns)
Change	Like keep up with subject	6	− (ns)	− (2%)	− (ns)	− (ns)	+ (ns)
	preparing . . . to build new society	8	− (ns)	− (1%)	− (ns)	− (ns)	− (5%)
	change young people's attitudes	18	− (ns)	+ (ns)	− (ns)	− (ns)	+ (5%)
	influence . . . to next generation	16	− (ns)	− (ns)	− (ns)	− (ns)	+ (ns)
Job	little danger of being out of job	19	+ (ns)	+ (2%)	+ (5%)	+ (1%)	+ (1%)
	pursue own hobbies in holidays	13	+ (ns)	+++ (ns)	+ (5%)	+++ (ns)	++ (2%)
	. . . have steady income	17	+ (ns)	+ (ns)	+ (5%)	+ (ns)	+ (0.1%)
	recuperate during holidays	15	+ (ns)	++ (10%)	+ (0.1%)	+ (2%)	++ (0.1%)
	can be fitted around other commitments	12	++ (ns)	++ (ns)	+ (0.1%)	+ (ns)	++ (0.1%)
Child-Self	Enjoy gaining confidence . . . of children	7	+ (10%)	− (ns)	+ (ns)	− (1%)	+ (1%)
Creativity-Challenge	increase . . . knowledge of myself	10	++ (ns)	++ (2%)	++ (ns)	++ (5%)	++ (10%)
	Enjoy doing something creative	2	+ (10%)	++ (2%)	+ (2%)	++ (0.1%)	+++ (0.1%)
	Enjoy challenge of situation	4	+ (ns)	+ (10%)	+ (10%)	+ (5%)	++ (ns)
	Like using talents to full	3	− (5%)	− (ns)	− (ns)	− (0.1%)	++ (ns)
Achievement (Children and Self)	guide child . . . suitable career	9	− (10%)	+ (ns)	− (ns)	+ (2%)	+ (ns)
	progress made by children	1	− (ns)	+ (0.1%)	− (ns)	+ (0.1%)	+ (ns)
	advancement in my career	14	− (ns)	− (ns)	− (ns)	− (ns)	− (ns)
Mixed	being with children . . . keep an open mind	10	+ (ns)	+ (ns)	− (ns)	+ (ns)	+ (ns)
	enjoy companionship of staffroom	20	+ (ns)	+ (ns)	− (ns)	+ (ns)	+ (ns)
	n =		58	58	27	132	98

Note: − ve sign denotes a decline in that 'reason for teaching' during the training year
+ ve sign denotes an increase in that 'reason for teaching' during the training year
Significance levels are recorded n.s. − not significant at 10% level
Source: TSRP (1973)

Table 5.7 *Rank order of items showing importance of various aspects of the course, at the beginning of the course. Change during the course plotted and direction of change marked*

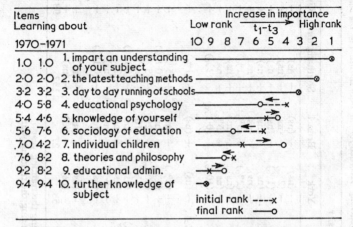

Items Learning about 1970–1971		Increase in importance Low rank t_1-t_3 High rank 10 9 8 7 6 5 4 3 2 1
1·0 1·0	1. impart an understanding of your subject	
2·0 2·0	2. the latest teaching methods	
3·2 3·2	3. day to day running of schools	
4·0 5·8	4. educational psychology	
5·4 4·6	5. knowledge of yourself	
5·6 7·6	6. sociology of education	
7·0 4·2	7. individual children	
7·6 8·2	8. theories and philosophy	
9·2 8·2	9. educational admin.	
9·4 9·4	10. further knowledge of subject	

initial rank ----x
final rank ——o

of the course either retain their importance (teaching methods and the day to day running of schools) or, like educational administration, increase in importance. The most remarkable change is in those items relating to knowledge of 'self' and of individual children. The stresses of the classroom situation and their first contacts with children cause these to be up-rated in practically all universities. The dedication to their teaching subject remains practically unchanged.

To conclude the discussion of this table it is perhaps worth taking the analysis one step further. Students come onto PGCE courses with a marked orientation, to teach their *subject*. There is a sense in which dedication to their own subject insulates students from the new perspective of the so-called theoretical aspects of the course. In addition to the above orientation, student teachers are becoming part of a teaching work force, that is, they actually go into classrooms and face classes of sometimes difficult children. In these circumstances some begin to adopt methods of dealing with classroom problems that run counter to their own ideals and bear a close similarity to the available role models within schools. At the same time, as student-teachers, they continue to be critical of existing practices within schools. Under these conflicting pressures some students are apt to show deeply felt opposition to critical perspectives which originate outside teaching. These perspectives bring with them additional problems often without solution and are posed by groups of people who do not have to face up to the practical day to day problems of the classroom. These criticisms often emerge within seminars with the question 'Why did *you* leave teaching?' For example, one frustrated and aggressive history student confronted her theory tutor with the question 'Why did you leave teaching – you would have had more influence if you had continued teaching and presented us with solutions not problems.'

Another area in which change measures were generated was the area of general attitudes to teaching and education discussed in Chapter 3. At this point it is relevant to add to Radicalism, Naturalism and Tendermindedness, the other two measures referred to earlier but not described.

Liberalism While this scale was initially conceived as a way of bringing the Oliver and Butcher (1965) Radicalism scale up-to-date. Later, we decided to bring in new issues as a separate scale. The new issues were: pupil participation (democracy), streaming (competition) and the issue of the unequal division of resources in favour of the poorer areas (compensation). These issues had been raised in the responses to an open ended pre-pilot questionnaire. A 'disagree' response to 'children learn best in a highly competitive situation' and an 'agree' response to 'older children should be allowed to make decisions in the running of the school' would score positively for 'Liberalism'.

Progressivism The *'relationships in teaching'* question was designed to measure those attitudes towards the teacher/pupil relationship that seemed to typify the Sussex approach. The items were generated from notes taken during seminars and at keynote lectures, and an attempt was made to select aspects of the teaching relationship that were stressed and occurred frequently. The six items have nevertheless been made as general as possible and they can be seen as containing two ideal types of teacher:

1 Child-centred or progressive teacher – a teacher who stresses good relationships more than academic results, social skills of teaching, remaining alive and aware, who is close and friendly and does not accept that distance or hostility as inevitable in the relationship with children.
2 Subject-centred or traditional teacher – a teacher who

111

stresses academic results, subject matter and the technical skills of teaching and accepts that distance in the relationship with children is necessary to be effective and that there is inevitably a certain amount of hostility.

We were aware of the possibility of built-in bias in this measure.

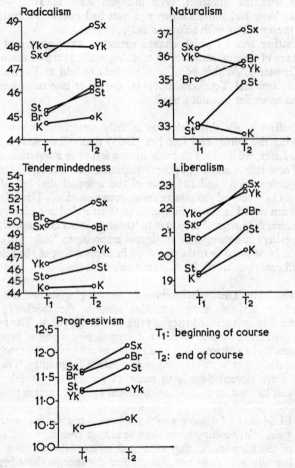

Source: TSRP (1973)

Figure 5.1

112

In looking at the final results, however, we found that it behaved very much like the other four scales. These five attitude scales were completed at the beginning and end of the course in all five universities. The results are summarized on facing p. 112. The over riding impression is of an increase in the mean score in these attitude scales at practically all universities. In all, 21 out of 25 scores move in an upward direction and only four, Naturalism at York and Kings, Radicalism at York and Tendermindedness at Brunel, move in a downward direction. The downward moves are all small and none are statistically significant. We can conclude that PGCE courses in general produce a social milieu in which the attitudes measured by this battery of scales are intensified in the student body, that is, students move towards being more Radical, more Naturalistic, etc.

There is one final strand of evidence that I would like to present before proceeding with a further discussion of the results.

Commitment to teaching

The examination of reasons for teaching leads logically to a consideration of commitment to teaching. We have seen that the PGCE courses produce a change in emphasis in the students' perception of their reasons for teaching. Career or job satisfaction increase while 'idealistic' or 'optimistic' reasons for teaching decline in importance. It is perhaps important to know if this process is linked with a change in students' overall commitment to teaching.

Students were asked at the beginning and end of their course if they would indicate their position on a scale (of commitment).

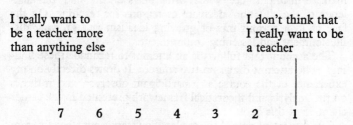

I really want to be a teacher more than anything else						I don't think that I really want to be a teacher
7	6	5	4	3	2	1

The result shows an overall high commitment to teaching but with some initial differences that are statistically significant.

Table 5.8 *Commitment to teaching – students' perceptions at beginning and end of course*

	Beginning	End	Diff.	Significance
Sussex	5·6	5·2	−0·41	2%
York	5·8	5·0	−0·83	0·1%
Brunel	5·5	5·1	−0·41	10%
Southampton	5·7	5·5	−0·26	1%
Kings	5·4	5·3	−0·03	ns

The changes recorded show a pattern of change very different from the Radicalism-Progressivism indicators. All universities record a decline in their commitment to teaching. It is Kings that shows the smallest decline and records the only non-significant change. At the other extreme, York students record a massive decline to move from being the most committed to the least committed.

One way of looking at this pattern is to notice that while it was the new universities that recorded the higher scores in the first instance, by the end of the course, the older universities showed the higher levels of commitment.

Some of the major indicators used in the study have now been reported. Enough has been said to reveal a number of apparently contradictory trends. On the one hand student-teachers in the sample show an increasing commitment to certain kinds of relationships within teaching and certain ways of teaching (Radicalism-Progressivism) and yet they all show a decline in their commitment to teaching as such. Under the heading 'reasons for teaching' they demonstrate that satisfactions like 'holidays' increase in importance, while 'using one's talents' and 'the challenge of the situation' decrease as reasons for teaching. On the face of it, a curious mix of growing idealism and growing disillusionment and lessening commitment.

The account that follows is an attempt to reconcile these findings. The attempt draws on two sources. It draws directly on my experience of the course as a participant observer, and it draws on the analysis and theoretical framework presented in the earlier chapters of this book.

One important part of the explanation stands out strongly from field work notes. Students found their teaching practice the most exhausting and engaging aspect of their course. 'When I come home on Wednesday night, it's plonk, I just collapse. I don't recover till Friday. Thursday is just like a weekend', is typical of many remarks recorded during seminars. Teaching absorbs all their mental and physical energy. It seems to require new skills, new approaches and new stances which they do not yet possess, and maybe do not agree with. In these circumstances, what appears to develop is an early split between attitudes relating to fairly general levels of education policy or teaching performance and more specific levels relating to their own experiences and their reasons for doing things. In the face of the evidence of their own exhaustion and, in some cases, a subjective assessment of their own lack of ability to cope, the importance of holidays, mind-freeing recreation and even job security become more attractive. At the same time, attractions like 'creative' and 'challenging' work and using 'talents to the full' decline steeply. Their own experience forces them to be far more modest in this direction. It may be they have not found the scope, it may be they doubt their own abilities, either way these items show collectively the steepest decline.

Attitudes at the more general level are not affected in the same way. Students do not yet feel part of the school system. At Sussex where students spend the largest period in schools they are as much influenced by university tutors as by school-based tutors and it is noticeable that on the general educational issues university tutors have most influence. It seems to be the surviving 'distance' from the school system, the critical awareness of its shortcomings, that enables general 'radical' and 'progressive' attitudes to grow relatively unaffected by specific experiences and situationally relevant strategies. It seems unlikely that this development could continue in the following year as students move into and take up positions as full-time teachers within the school system.

The phenomena that I have called 'displacing the blame' is more likely to be a radical displacement of blame when the individual feels less part of and responsible for the system. The more rewards the teacher accepts within the school system during his/her career the more difficult it becomes to see themselves apart from it. Indeed in the next chapter we will examine situations in which teachers find it necessary to accept and present themselves in terms of the system in order to compete for these rewards, for example, scaled allowances, and head of department allowances. The pressures on the individual to move the displacement of blame from a radical direction to an establishment direction increase during a teacher's career. The reaction to these pressures remains an individual response.

The decrease in commitment to teaching is therefore not inconsistent with an increase in Radicalism but it is a process we might expect to change.

Differentiation within the process of student-teacher socialization

In our previous discussion of commitment, we pointed out that there was a certain amount of danger in using the term because the everyday use of the word makes it appear unambiguously a 'good thing' to have. The purpose of the discussion that follows is to tease out some of the possible meanings of this finding in two directions, (1) commitment to what sort of teaching (i.e. in what sort of school), (2) commitment to teaching for what reasons? In order to simplify this discussion we will trace the argument for only two universities, Sussex and Kings, which were the two universities most different from each other in our original design.

The selection of university departments of education for study was an important aspect of the original research. It was carried out by Mary Horton and described in detail in the research report (1973). The universities were selected along two dimensions; student choice, recorded by the Graduate Teacher Training Registry; and course structure, as recorded in the handbook of the course. In each dimension an example of a department 'most like' Sussex and one 'least like' Sussex was chosen. The following table sets out the results of the selection:

Table 5.9 *Course structure*

		Most like Sussex	Least like Sussex
Student choices (recorded by students who also chose Sussex)	Most like Sussex	York	Southampton
	Least like Sussex	Brunel	Kings (London)

1 *Commitment-type of teaching* It became clear in an examination of university differences that Kings stood within a different tradition of teacher education. Its students were recruited to a greater extent from the independent and direct grant system. They were more likely to have attended the older universities and come to the course with markedly different orientations and attitudes.

116

They were more likely to spend their period of teaching practice within the direct grant system so it was to be expected that their commitment to teaching was largely a commitment to teaching within schools with selective intakes. By the time the final questionnaire was administered to Kings students, 73 per cent had arranged teaching jobs and 48 per cent were in independent, direct grant or grammar schools. This contrasts with Sussex and Brunel, where 71 per cent and 60 per cent respectively had taken appointments and only 16 per cent and 13 per cent had taken appointments in selective schools. If these differences had been small it would have been possible to argue that the commitment measure was recording an orientation to a similar career. The differences are in fact so large that 'commitment to teaching' means something rather different in the two contexts.

The graphs on pages 118–19 show that these differences have been sustained throughout the careers of the students at Kings and Sussex.

2 Reasons for commitment In order to begin to understand 'commitment to teaching', we produced a large correlation matrix in which commitment scores were related to a large number of grouped variables used in the analysis. An examination of this matrix quickly revealed a set of items positively related to commitment and interestingly enough *negatively* related to the radicalism-progressivism attitudes. The items that were positively related quickly produced a picture (see table below on pp. 122–3) similar to that found by Robert Merton (1957) in his study of medical students and their decision to become doctors.

A youthful decision (which is characteristic of medicine) is generally a more enthusiastic one. Other occupations are seldom considered seriously; doubts about whether a medical career is the right choice are relatively infrequent; and, on entrance into medical school, the chosen profession seems like the only one that could be satisfactory. Students who pick their careers at an early age were also more likely to be influenced and encouraged by their families, and less likely to be helped by contemporaries.

The correlation coefficients show that committed *teachers* chose teaching early and they saw their subject as an important reason for teaching. They were satisfied with teaching and assessed their

They were more likely to spend their period of teaching practice
within the their grant system so it was to be expected that their
commitment to teaching was largely ... ion nearer to teaching
within schools with effective ranked. By the time the final questionnaire was administered to s ... ..., only 28 per cent had
arranged ... ... in independent
direct-grant or grammar schools. ... comes ... in comprehensive
Brunel, while 71 per cent and 60 per cent respectively had left a
appren ... and of the job, cent and 58 per cent ... ...
apprentices in comprehensive schools. If these differences had been
small it would be justifiable to ... ...
amounts were according so that there were significantly ... The
differences are in fact so large ... ...unlikely that ... ...
means that by ... the children at the two points ...
The graphs on pages Fig. 18 show that these figures have
b ... ... comparison, the ... of the student at Kings
and ...

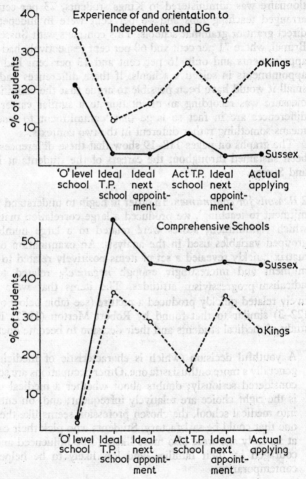

Experience of and orientation to
Independent and DG

Comprehensive Schools

Kings
Sussex

'O' level school | Ideal T.P. school | Ideal next appointment | Act T.P. school | Ideal next appointment | Actual applying

Figure 5.2 (Pt. I)

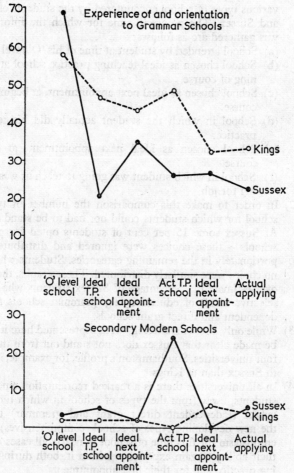

Source: TSRP (1973)

Figure 5.2 (Pt. II)

Notes to Fig 5.2

(1) These graphs describe the experiences of and orientations to various types of school encountered by the students of Kings and Sussex. The points in time for which the information was gathered are as follows:
   (a) School attended by student at time of his 'O' level exams.
   (b) School chosen as ideal teaching practice school at beginning of course.
   (c) School chosen as ideal next appointment, at beginning of course.
   (d) School in which the student actually did his teaching practice.
   (e) School chosen as ideal next appointment, at end of course.
   (f) School in which student was going to teach or was applying for job.

(2) In order to make this comparison the number of types of school for which students could opt had to be standardized. At Sussex some 15 per cent of students opted for primary schools – these choices were ignored and distributed proportionately in the remaining categories. Students who make no choice were similarly distributed. These graphs, therefore, over-estimate the percentage of Sussex students who choose selective forms of education, e.g. grammar schools and independent and direct grant schools.

(3) While only Sussex and Kings were represented here it should be made clear that Sussex does not stand out from the other four universities. Southampton's profile, for example, is closer to Sussex than to Kings.

(4) In all universities there is a marked reorientation among the students, away from the types of school in which they were taught (independent direct grant and grammar) towards the new developing types of school (comprehensives). Their enthusiasm for this type of school in nearly all cases outruns their ability to gain experience within it, both during teaching practice and for their first appointment.

teaching ability highly. In other words, they appear to have the sort of professional commitment that resembles that of doctors, who choose their profession very early and show high levels of commitment and satisfaction. It is interesting to note that the 'committed' teacher chose to take Cert.Ed. because it offered prospects of a better career and, at Kings, students who have family connections with teaching are high in commitment. This family background characteristic is mentioned by Merton and is important in medicine and law but is not usually believed to be so in teaching.

In the light of this evidence it seems reasonable to suggest two broad streams of motivation to teach. One is the professional commitment to teach in which the student has the positive characteristics described above but is also recognizably not 'Radical-Progressive' in his views of education. In the other, the student is committed to a set of ideals about education and society, he is *not* committed to teaching as such and, in so far as he is blocked from realizing his ideals through teaching, is prepared to explore other means of bringing them about.

Table 5.10 on pages 122–3 shows the extent to which characteristics of 'committed' teachers are either not shared or rejected by 'radical-progressive' teachers.

Radicals are clearly not subject-orientated, they choose teaching late rather than early, they are not satisfied with teaching (but not markedly dissatisfied either), they tend to rate their ability low and have low academic and teaching self concepts. On the other hand, they are interested in teaching in certain types of school. The correlations in the bottom section of the table use a scale in which comprehensive schools are given a score of 3 and opposed to grammar, direct grant and independent schools, which are given a score of 1. The positive correlations with the Radicalism-Progressivism scales therefore indicate a desire to teach in this type of school. The most important finding here, however, is in the last line of the table where it is clear that radicals *actually teach* in comprehensive schools after leaving the course. Professionally committed teachers do not, on the other hand, choose any type of school preferentially (i.e. more than the rest of their university cohort).

A suggestion made in this analysis has been that professionally committed teachers see themselves as committed to teaching *per se*, that is, committed to a career in the classroom and the school. The radical commitment sees teaching as a means rather than an end and, in so far as teaching proves an ineffectual means, it will be deserted for other, more effective means either in education or outside. We are able to test this assertion because we asked

Table 5.10 Table of correlation coefficients between commitment on the one hand and R, N, T, P and L on the other with a variety of descriptive variables

Sussex	Commitment T_1	Radical-Progressive Rad.	Nat.	Tend.	Prog.	Lib.
Subject orientation (RFT)	-0.16	-0.12	-0.17	-0.21	-0.04	-0.17
Chose teaching early	0.55*	0.05	-0.12	-0.12	-0.20	-0.30*
Satisfied with teaching as career	0.59*	0.07	0.04	-0.17	-0.03	-0.03
Self-assessed ability (teaching)	0.15	-0.16	-0.24	0.25*	-0.18	-0.13
Family connections and teaching	0.02	0.02				
Chose Cert.Ed. because gave prospects of better career	0.16	-0.35*	-0.28*	-0.22	-0.40*	-0.39*
Academic-self concept	0.82*	0.09	0.00	-0.17	-0.17	-0.10
Teaching-self concept	0.22	0.20	-0.33*	-0.37*	-0.17	-0.37*
Radicalism	0.11					
Naturalism	-0.22					
Tendermindedness	-0.04					
Progressivism	-0.13					
Liberalism	-0.10					
Type of School 1. For TP	0.09	0.07	-0.08	-0.10	0.02	0.35*
2. Ideal first job	0.02	0.40*	0.31*	0.12	0.24	0.52*
3. Actual job (T_2)		0.44*	0.30*	0.15	-0.09	0.30*

121

Kings	Commitment	Radical-Progressive T_1				
	T_1	Rad.	Nat.	Tend.	Prog.	Lib.
Subject orientation (RFT)	0·35*	-0·00	-0·30*	-0·26*	-0·01	-0·14
Chose teaching early	0·55*	-0·19	-0·28*	-0·23*	-0·09	-0·11
Satisfied with teaching as career	0·33*	-0·11	-0·05	-0·03	-0·09	-0·08
Self-assessed ability (teaching)	0·33*	-0·07	-0·20*	-0·22*	-0·09	-0·13
Family connections with teaching	0·27*					
Chose Cert.Ed. because gave prospects of better career	0·36*	-0·07	-0·21*	-0·28*	-0·06	-0·16
Academic-self concept	0·20*	-0·01	0·01	0·01	0·22*	-0·03
Training-self concept	0·40*	0·01	-0·09	-0·19	-0·12	-0·04
Radicalism	-0·09					
Naturalism	-0·20*					
Tendermindedness	-0·15					
Progressivism	0·07					
Liberalism	-0·10					
Type of School 1. For TP	-0·15	0·20*	0·18	0·21*	0·13	0·28*
2. For ideal job	-0·02	0·30*	0·24*	0·29*	0·14	0·26*
3. Actual job (T_2)		0·14	0·19	0·16	0·06	0·63*

Source: TSRP (1973)

Notes to Table 5.10

1 In all instances, indicators measured at T_1 are correlated with other measures from T_1.
2 *marks all correlation coefficients with less than 5 per cent chance of occurring randomly.
3 The large number of significant correlations on both sides of the dividing line show that the differences we are examining are quite marked. We have not, for example, used the less rigorous statistical tests for differences between pairs of correlation coefficients which would have demonstrated an even larger number of differences at the 5 per cent level.
4 The table is arranged so that expected positive and expected negative correlations occur together in the four quartiles of the table. Inspection shows that, while some correlations are not in the expected direction, only one at Kings and one at Sussex occur at the 5 per cent level.

students what type of work they hoped to be doing in the future (say, in about fifteen years' time). The question listed the following options:

1 Teaching in a school
2 School head or deputy
3 Teaching in further education (including technical colleges)
4 Teaching in research in higher education (university, polytechnic, college of education)
5 Educational administration (including educational psychology)
6 Other employment (please specify)
7 Housewife
8 No idea

When the specifications of 'other employment' were examined for Sussex students, it was found that *all* respondents who were prepared to make forecasts envisaged remaining within education. The following tabulations for Sussex are simplified so that categories 1 and 2 (a career within teaching or the school) are set against 3–6 (a career inside education but outside the school).

The pattern is clear. Committed teachers are far more likely to see their careers within schools. Liberals are more likely to see their careers in the broader spectrum of education.

Table 5.11 *Showing the relationship between commitment and future career –
Sussex*

Commitment	Future Career		
	Career within School	Career within Education (outside school)	Total
High	19	10	29
Medium	5	10	15
Low	2	13	15
Total	26	33	59

$$\chi^2 = 12{\cdot}79 \quad df = 2 \quad p < 0{\cdot}01$$

Showing the relationship between liberalism and future career – Sussex

Liberalism	Future Career		
	Career within School	Career within Education (outside school)	Total
High	8	19	27
Medium	7	8	15
Low	10	4	14
Total	25	31	56

$$\chi^2 = 7{\cdot}07 \quad df = 2 \quad p < 0{\cdot}01$$

Conclusion

The presentation of change data in this section has been an
attempt to broaden the basis of the comparison of outcomes between the courses at the five universities. The results make it clear
that the universities we are considering represent a spectrum
within the broader process of teacher education. However, the
spectrum is complex and not uni-dimensional so that simple
categorical conclusions are not in keeping with the data. Even a
relatively simple idea like 'commitment to teaching' needs qualification and careful examination.

The analysis leads to a finding of a sufficiently high level of
generality to be presented in a conceptually simple and clear way.
The presentation of the change data on 'commitment' and its

contrast with the change data on the 'Radicalism-Progressivism' attitudes led us to make a set of more detailed contrasts. The technique revealed two broad streams of commitment to education within the student bodies we examined (Sussex and Kings). The first, more obvious form of commitment was to a career in teaching (a subject) and schools, which was similar in many ways to commitment in the older professions, for example medicine and law. This was strong at Kings and weak at Sussex. The second form of commitment was to education in its broadest form and to a set of ideals which might be realized through education. Students with this second form of commitment see teaching as a means rather than an end and are only loosely committed to teaching as such. This was strong at Sussex and weak at Kings. They acquire jobs in the schools which they feel will give them the freedom to teach in the ways they wish (comprehensive schools) and already see their careers taking them outside the classroom and outside the school.

The importance of this finding is underlined by the fact that, taking the sample as a whole, slightly less than 40 per cent of students expect to be teaching or in schools as heads or deputy heads within fifteen years of leaving the course.

The implications of these findings are far-reaching for the design of post-graduate certificate courses. They must increasingly be seen as dual or perhaps multi-purpose qualifications which could contain options on which later specializations could be built. Certainly they are already seen very differently by the broad streams of 'radical' and 'professionally committed' students.

The implications of these findings for a theory of socialization are also far reaching. We have been able to lift out from the evidence two broad strands of socialization, which according to our analysis represent options that student-teachers can adopt and explore. There is no question of a single mode of adaptation to the institutions concerned, the school or the university. We have also seen that students are able to affect their own socialization by their initial choice of university and then by making choices within the course.

The differences described have been illustrated using attitude measures, but the pattern that emerges dovetails closely with the picture developed from the participant observation data in Chapter 3. Chapter 3 brings an understanding of the choices open to student-teachers and the process that gives rise to the pattern of attitude change. For example, we saw that students are able to adopt different strategies within the course. For some this results in acceptance of the institution's norms (internalized adjustment) but for others this results in conflict (strategic redefinition). Others protect themselves from institutional pressures (strategic compliance).

In the last two chapters we have examined the central tendency in the socialization process – the functional theory emphasis – and we have teased out from that process alternative and conflicting modes – the conflict theory emphasis – and have examined situational constraints and micro processes – the interpretive-symbolic interactionist emphasis. In addition we have illustrated the scope for creative action and choice – the sociology of the possible emphasis.

This chapter began by pointing to the important connection between socialization and social change. We traced the connection using the idea of social strategy and pointed out that actors can produce change both by creating new strategies and by making choices within already existing options. The existence of the 'radical' strand of socialization within teacher training therefore means that there is considerable scope for change. If succeeding cohorts of student-teachers opt more for one strand rather than another, considerable change can take place.

It is important not to overemphasize the importance of the student-teacher culture. When students leave the course to take up their first appointments student-teacher culture becomes a latent culture. We have already looked at many of the disjunctions in this transition, reported by researchers in the 60s and 70s, so we can expect many aspects of that culture to come under pressure and disappear. On the other hand we must not be simplistic in interpreting rapid adaptation to the new and pressing circumstances of a first job. Strategic compliance is an important concept and needs investigating in this new situation.

Chapter 6

The career

The plunge

The first year of teaching is like the first swim across the deep end of the pool, like the first solo drive through London traffic after passing the driving test. The teacher emerges from his training conscious that the worst is over but by no means sure that the improvements will be rapid. As with the impact of teaching practice, the new teachers find themselves almost swamped by a flood of events; teaching material, much of which, if new, has to be prepared; pupils' work needs to be marked; classes have to be met on time and taught; a sea of new faces, events and procedures have to be memorized and stored for future use. The ideas and skills developed during the training year are found to be inadequate for the new task and the new responsibilities.

There are, now, a number of new ingredients in the situation compared to the training year which we should note. Although they are still 'probationary' teachers and will not achieve qualified teacher status until the end of the year, the probation is in most cases nominal. The 'student' status has gone and they are members of the profession. Their protected status has gone, and indeed for some, their junior status in a school will mean that they

128

are given the most difficult teaching assignments. They will be influenced by the fact that they can start to establish themselves in the school and in the profession.

This chapter falls naturally into two sections. In the first section, the beginning teachers are allowed to speak for themselves and I attempt a structured presentation of their own reported impressions. The structure is necessary to allow some forty pages of reported material to be condensed into about a dozen quotations. It also links this chapter with earlier discussions of the two broad streams of socialization located in the training year – the radical and the professional. The structure forms a basis for the interpretation of the material.

The second section rounds off the book with an account of teacher socialization in a small grammar school. This account is based on a functional model of the socialization process and as such attracts some criticism. The purpose of the account is to introduce a conventional view of some of the major constraints and career pressures in teaching, while bearing in mind that alternative research perspectives have yet to be applied to this area.

The data used in the first section of this chapter is derived from a follow-up questionnaire study of student teachers from Sussex and Southampton. Most of the analysis rests on the Sussex data, but the conclusions are confirmed by the work done on the Southampton material. We will continue to illustrate the two major themes within the socialization process: on the one hand, the general trends and changes that influence the whole cohort; on the other hand, the differentiating experiences and responses of a group of people making choices and trying to control some aspects of their own development and the institutions in which they work.

In the last chapter a number of predictions were made about the general impact of the first job. In particular, we examined trends in general attitudes to education that had developed during the training period and predicted reversals in a number of them. These were borne out in the survey for both Sussex and Southampton.

The graphs on p. 130 show that in the four attitude scales measured at three separate times (the beginning of the course, the end of the course and the end of the first year of teaching) T_1, T_2, and T_3, the scores plunge to about their original level. Conversely, for those remaining in teaching commitment scores increase abruptly. It would appear that after only one year of training, the new teachers are seeing themselves more definitely as members of the profession and less convinced by the idealistic stances of yesterday.

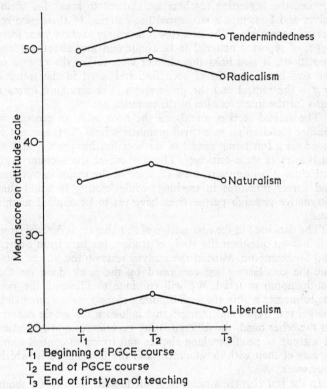

Figure 6.1 *Four attitude scales plotted at T_1, T_2, and T_3 – Sussex PGCE*

The general impression obtained from the graphs is borne out by the answers to an open-ended question which asked respondents to describe the ways they felt their 'views on education' had changed since finishing the PGCE course. Some edited versions of these answers are presented here. They are arranged so that they also illustrate the second theme: differentiation. The quotations are arranged so that the remarks made by the radical teachers are juxtaposed with those made by the more traditionally committed teachers. There are high correlations between all the Radical-Progressive indicators. The most up to date and educationally relevant indicator is the Liberalism score. This score is therefore used in this section as an indicator of general radical-progressive attitudes. Liberalism scores of 22 and above are above the mean.

Many respondents were agreed that the education system was in a bad state; their views on the causes and remedies were often dramatically at variance.

I now feel that only quite radical change will improve the education system. I can quite happily continue to teach my academic subject in a reasonable academic way, but with little response from the children. Only when there is a complete restructuring of the curriculum will anything change really for the better.
(George B. A French teacher in a grammar school. Liberalism score 25)

Compare with:

I did not realise what a state education is in, thanks to unthinking innovation.
(Kathleen B. A primary school teacher. Liberalism score 13)

Most respondents also agreed that the main teaching problems were posed by socially disadvantaged, less able pupils, but once again the remedies that were suggested differed widely.

... the technical aspects of English language seem to be quite irrelevant – discussion and encouragement of self-confidence through oral work based on any interesting subject seems to be the most practially useful activity for them ...
... I have become less idealistic about imparting anything but a transitory 'love of literature' ... teaching must be a preparation for life ... they are at odds with the function of the school as a whole, which is imparting academic knowledge. Do many schools really have a policy relevant to all regarding the aims of education?
(Margaret B. An English teacher in a comprehensive school. Liberalism score 28)

131

The remedy for some less radical students was the complete exclusion of the most difficult category of pupil.

> Raising the school leaving age to 16 is a bad idea. Education and training should be available for those who are prepared to work for it.
> (Chemistry teacher in a grammar school/6th form college. Liberalism score 20)

and:

> ... education ... influenced by non-practising theorists, who stress child-centred education at the expense of teacher-centred education. The best example of this is ROSLA, which forces children and teachers into a situation of great stress without the slightest regard for the reality of the situation.
> (French teacher in a comprehensive school. Liberalism score 14)

As we have seen in our earlier analysis, the 'reality of the situation' depends very much on who views the situation: the intersection of biography and situation. The agreement on the existence of a problem is destroyed immediately the diagnosis begins about the nature of the problem. As before, that is when they were students, the radical teachers tend to see the problems emerging from the school or the staff; the traditional teachers see problems emerging from the pupils.

> My emphasis on the personal relationship with kids has increased as a reaction against the views prevailing (as far as I can see) on the staff.
> (French teacher in a grammar school. Liberalism score 27)

Compared with:

> ... there creeps in some uncertainty about the true benefit of the greater freedom, when I see some traits which are *also* appearing: 1. A questioning mind it seems is only a step from a cynical one; and 2. I begin to realize that humility is a virtue, but it does not co-exist with self-confidence; not at least in our young.
> (French teacher in a grammar school. Liberalism score 14)

Once the diagnosis moves on to proposing solutions, the differences multiply. The radical teachers tend to see the problems as the responsibility of the 'system' and the 'teacher', and propose solutions to make the teacher/pupil relationship closer. The traditional teachers tend to see the problem as residing more with the child. The relationship with the child should therefore become more structured, more easily understood and enforced by discipline (sanctions, including exclusion) rather than an emotional tie. First the radical teacher:

> I have come to feel that the more time you spend with a class the better you know them and can anticipate their likely needs and responses. One double period a week seems to get me nowhere fast, particularly with children in the throes of 'growing up' who are otherwise preoccupied most of the time.
> I teach about 350 pupils per week and this is far too many. I would much prefer to teach an integrated science course and have fewer pupils to deal with. I have found that the classes I see most are those I cater for best, whether or not they are 'good' classes.
> (Chemistry teacher in a comprehensive school. Liberalism score 26)

It is in trying to develop the close supportive relationship that many radical teachers experience their greatest difficulty.

> ... With my own form I have tried to be extremely close, as I feel every child should have at least one teacher to whom he can turn without worry about getting into trouble. Unfortunately this has led to a few discipline problems in the classroom situation. My particular dilemma is that although I still adhere to my principle as regards my own form's pastoral difficulties it is vital that strict discipline is maintained when I am teaching. I teach a particularly dangerous subject [chemistry] ... will have to try again next year.
> (Chemistry teacher in a comprehensive school. Liberalism score 25)

In contrast:

> I am very disillusioned with progressive ideas on education and methods. By this I refer to the modern attitudes towards

discipline and pastoral care. I am not referring to progressive education in terms of syllabus changes, e.g. I favour Nuffield Science methods ...

... the student-teachers are given far too much freedom by university staff. More discipline and a stricter programme of compulsory learning is needed, more respect would then be the product ...

I have found that the children I teach at the moment and also student-teachers on the Cert.Ed. course at Sussex learn best (in general) in disciplined structured systems.

(Chemistry teacher in a comprehensive school. Liberalism score 13)

The last respondent, in common with many others, records his reaction to his experience as though it represents a major change in his views, 'I am very disillusioned ...' In fact, our record of these teachers/student-teachers over the two years of the PGCE course and the probationary teaching year shows that really large changes in their views of education are unusual. The large shifts of mean values on the 'Radicalism', 'Naturalism', etc, indicators were caused by relatively small shifts of opinion in the large majority of student-teachers. In the Liberalism score, for example, only 29 per cent of student-teachers recorded a drop in their score. Twice that percentage recorded upward movement. In the case of the last respondent, our records show that at all times, the beginning of the course, the end of the course, and the end of his first year of teaching, he would have been classified in the least radical category (Liberalism scores 18, 17, 13). In other words, his sense of disillusionment was experienced within this least radical category.

If we examine the movement of the whole group over this two year period between, say, three categories, high (radical), medium and low (traditional), we find that only 27 per cent of respondents changed category, and none moved from the highest to the lowest or vice versa. The results are summarized in the table on p. 135.

Where unusually large changes occur they are frequently associated with unusually severe or extreme teaching situations. It is illustrative to examine two of these cases.

Michael A., an English teacher, showed the largest decline recorded on the Liberalism scale (L.30 at the end of the course to L.21 after one year's teaching). He wrote:

I am afraid that many of my views have changed radically as a result of teaching in an extremely tough immigrant school. Furthermore (I have taught in two schools in the area) I have been allotted only 3rd and 4th year bottom stream children. My opinion from the head down (barring two teachers) of the staff is that they are indifferent and incompetent and quite unable to deal with the problems of the schools. I think that I am probably too close to the situation at present to write anything really useful – whatever I write would be simply bitter, unpleasant and would only reflect my complete dis-affection with the situation.

He saw himself as moving out of school teaching into F.E. and then journalism.

Table 6.1 *Changes in the Liberalism score between the beginning of the course and the end of the first year of teaching*

| | | Liberalism score at end of 1st year, T_3 | | | |
		High	Medium	Low	Total T_1
Liberalism score at beginning of course, T_1	High	8	2	0	10
	Medium	4	9	3	16
	Low	0	6	9	15
	Total T_3	12	17	12	41

The results are borne out in all the similar attitude measures (N, R, T & P).

On the other hand, Arabella S., a physics teacher, recorded one of the largest gains. During the course she moved from a score of L.14 to L.25. After a year's teaching in a small girls' grammar school she maintained this level of Radicalism (24), and wrote:

A year's teaching in a small girls' grammar school has made me realize that even a large comprehensive [teaching practice school] is better than the narrow-minded institutions that exist in some authorities. I feel much more comprehensive inclined and mixed ability inclined and know that in looking for my next job I shall aim for a small comprehensive (c. 1000) with a wide range of courses for low and high ability children. At my teaching practice school I felt very right wing, at my present post I am accused of being very left wing. I now agree with many opinions about education I disagreed with during my course.

It is apparent that the streams of socialization that we identified as a characteristic of the student-teacher culture continue and flow on into schools. It is true that the problems of the classroom compel the new teachers to take on a new perspective. The student culture has now become a latent culture providing a reservoir of skills and values on which the probationary teacher can draw. In addition, new strategies have to be selected, learned or created to support the new teacher in his/her new situation. What we have seen in the quotations from the teachers' own reports is that many strategies are seen to be less appropriate than before but there is still no agreement, no consensus. The school has now become the arena for competing pressures. On the one hand there is the need to become effective and accepted within the school, on the other hand the desire to make the school more like the place in which the teacher would like to teach. In some cases these competing pressures cannot be reconciled. The creativity of the new teacher is simply not up to the task, and strategic compliance strategies are not broad enough to bridge the gap. In the cases we have examined, Arabella will leave the constricting atmosphere of the small town grammar school to find what she thought would be a more open and challenging comprehensive school; Michael will leave what he experienced as the chaotic and exhausting atmosphere of the inner city comprehensive for a college of further education or journalism.

The view of socialization that we have pursued now gives us a new way of looking at institutions (schools). Instead of viewing them as relatively homogenous institutions simply absorbing the 'barbaric invaders' and turning them into exact replicas of pre-existing role holders, we can see them also as institutions penetrated by a flow of individuals who hold divergent views as to how the institution should be run, indeed, as to what the purpose of the institution is! These tensions are reconciled, but they remain as subterranean issues, part of the backcloth against which other dramas are enacted and other battles (such as interdepartmental issues) are fought out. Very, very occasionally these subterranean issues erupt to bring the very existence of the school into question. We will elaborate on this way of looking at schools later in this section.

There is unfortunately no study of a school with this theoretical perspective as its point of departure. The structures and concerns of the school have been assumed to be sufficiently stable to absorb the creative energies of new staff and divert them to other ends. The departmental structure, the pastoral structure and the career concerns that young teachers soon develop have been assumed sufficient to account for the socialization of young teachers. This functional model once again falls short of explaining the change that has taken place in our schools over the last 15 years. It overlooks, for example, the way the individual teacher can select schools in which he/she can try new ideas, and the possibility that where this fails a teacher can comply with an uncongenial regime for many years until the ideas that have remained untried become possibilities.

The new teacher is preoccupied with the basic problems of survival and acceptance. The strain of being 'new' is in itself considerable. As the newness wears off, that is, as many of the appropriate behaviour patterns are learned and habitualized, these strains are reduced. The energies released enable the young teacher to 'try again' on some of the preferred but unsuccessful teaching strategies of the first year. But once again there are competing pressures and choices to be made. As the pattern of career advancement becomes clearer and the expectations of the established senior staff are communicated, these expectations become pressures that must be taken into account.

Certainly one of the Sussex respondents found career pressures obtruding even in his first year of teaching. The young teacher reported below is assisting in an attempt to introduce an 'A' level Environmental Studies as a step towards integrating subjects and staff.

My views on education have not changed very much since leaving Sussex. I feel like the proverbial small cog and realise that education, like some other professions, is a rat-race for promotion. At the moment, being unmarried I feel that I am free of some of the pressure that can be brought to bear on some of the staff (i.e. by heads of departments).

(A biology teacher in a technical school. Liberalism score 27). It is interesting to note that as a 'radical' teacher he sees career

137

pressures as something to hold out against. It will be remembered that professionally committed teachers (who were not likely to be radicals) gave the prospect of a better career as an important reason for choosing to do the certificate in education. It seems probable that they would not define conversations and advice from senior staff as constituting an unwelcomed pressure, but as simply constituting helpful advice. There were, however, no reports in the questionnaire returns that illustrate this.

The career

In the last section of this chapter I describe a case study of teacher socialization in a grammar school. It is taken from a piece of research that I completed over ten years ago. I therefore refer to patterns of socialization that are dated – the main fieldwork period was between 1962 and 1965. The description highlights many of the developments in a teacher's career and the considerable constraints that affect the selection of appropriate strategies at each stage in that career.

In this research the major concern of the researcher was to document the way teacher socialization interacted with the processes of differentiation and polarization within the pupil body. The researcher confined himself to mapping the broad outline of the professional socialization process and he did not make problematic the notion that there was *one* such process. I feel it is worth including for two reasons: (1) the account is unbalanced because it is deficient in certain important respects, not because it distorts the data that is reported; (2) it is possible to illustrate from more recent data some of these deficiencies, and in doing so it will be possible to make a number of important theoretical and methodological points. Before introducing the case study it is therefore important to see whether the two broad streams of socialization we have identified within the student-teacher phase and the first year of teaching continue into the later period of the teaching career. In the course of the Tutorial Schools Research Project, data was collected on a sample of practising teachers in mid-career, the teacher-tutors, as well as a sample of teachers from the same schools. This sample was selected by matching the teacher-tutors on two dimensions, seniority and subject. The control sample was selected to see if the Sussex scheme selected teachers or influenced them to become more Radical, Naturalistic, etc. The results of the comparison are shown below.

Table 6.2 *The mean scores of teacher-tutors and their control groups on Naturalism, Radicalism and Tendermindedness*

	Naturalism	Radicalism	Tender-mindedness	
Tutors	32·8	46·1	43·7	$n = 35$
Controls	29·5	41·8	39·7	$n = 21$
Difference	3·3	4·3	4·0	$N = 56$
t-test	2·09	2·37	1·70	
Level of significance Tutors v. controls	$p < 0.05$	$p < 0.05$	$p < 0.01$	

Source: TSRP (1973)

The differences were consistent across subject groups, where once again the English teachers emerged as most Radical, etc. It would seem likely that the major element in this difference occurred through the selection of teacher-tutors, but the research was unable to substantiate this.

The member of the Tutorial Research Project team, Peter Hoad, who conducted this aspect of the research, noted that teacher-tutors themselves differed considerably in their style of supervision of student-teachers. Some saw their role as mainly integrating the student into the social and academic life of the school, while others saw their major responsibility as the allocating of duties to and assessing the teaching performance of their students. The diagnosis of these different elements of the teacher-tutor role occurred during a series of interviews with teacher-tutors, and this was followed up by including a series of questions in a teacher-tutor questionnaire. The results of this questionnaire are of interest to us here because the styles of tutoring that emerge correspond fairly closely with the styles that would be expected to emerge from the broad streams of socialization that we have been considering. The questionnaire asked tutors to rank six items (1 to 6) in order of importance in tutoring Sussex student-teachers. (See Table 6.3).

Peter Hoad noticed that, while nearly all tutors agreed on the importance of items 1 and 2, there was no consensus on items 3, 4 and 5. Tutors that ranked item 5 high tended not to rank item 4 high, and in addition a distinct category of tutors ranking item 3 high began to emerge. On the basis of this questionnaire three groups of tutors were arranged – 'Integrators', 'Allocators' and 'Assessors' – and the characteristics of their reported

Table 6.3 *Tutors' ranking of activities (Teacher-Tutor Questionnaire)*

Item	1	2	3	4	5	6
1. Giving practical advice	26	6	3	1	0	1
2. Giving encouragement	20	8	4	2	2	0
*3. Varying the teaching load	9	4	9	10	3	1
*4. Integrating into school	4	5	6	8	9	4
*5. Assessing students	7	2	2	9	9	7
6. Giving theoretical ideas	2	0	4	9	8	13

(N.B. Rank 1 was over used by respondents, who sometimes gave rank 1 to two items.)
Source: TSRP (1973)

tutoring styles were examined in some detail. For example, during tutorials integrators tended to be spontaneous in the selection of topics for discussion, while allocators followed a check list. Assessors placed the least emphasis on tutorials but most on supervision. Integrators were the most flexible with respect to student-requested change of timetable activity, assessors were the least flexible. The students of integrator tutors recorded the highest gains in two aspects of adjustment while at the teaching practice school, particularly informal adjustment; the students of assessor tutors recorded a loss in informal adjustment scores but the highest gain on formal adjustment. It would appear that the Sussex teacher-tutors were practising distinctly different tutorial styles and that these differences were noticed by and had an effect upon their students. We would expect that these practices stem from differences in deep-seated views on education. It was possible to examine this question through the Naturalism, Radicalism and Tendermindedness scores of the tutors.

Table 6.4 *Tutors' styles and their opinions on education as measured on Naturalism, Radicalism and Tendermindedness scales*

Styles	Mean Scores		
	Naturalism	Radicalism	Tendermindedness
Integrators	36·1	49·0	48·7
Allocators	30·9	45·1	42·7
Assessors	30·25	43·9	39·0
t-test	2·954	2·234	3·599
(Int.–Assess.)	$p < 0.05$	$p < 0.05$	$p < 0.05$

Source: TSRP (1973)

The integrators are clearly more Naturalistic, Radical and Tenderminded, and although the differences between assessors and allocators are not statistically significant, the assessors are in all cases at the opposite pole to the integrators. It would appear that even in mid-career teachers exhibit important differences in pedagogic strategies (at least those appropriate to student-teachers) that are consistent with their attitudes to education. This example must be seen only as illustrative, since we were unable to pursue these differences into the classroom. The new range of constraints that are operative within the classroom might well result in less noticeable divergences in pedagogic style.

To summarize the argument, if we assume that every cohort of student-teachers presents the broad spectrum of opinions on education that characterized the group being studied, our analysis predicts that while a young teacher will be concerned about doing the right things in order to become, say, a head of department, he will *also* be concerned about the *kind* of head of department he can become, for example, whether or not he will be able to put his ideals into practice. Those who feel that the constraints of the job are unacceptable are more likely to leave teaching for other occupations. As we saw in Chapter 5, it is those teachers who score high on Liberalism who anticipate feeling blocked and expect to leave teaching for other jobs in education during the first fifteen years of their career. Certainly the expansion of areas of colleges of education, departments of education and curriculum development projects during the 1960s will have absorbed a large number of teachers who (if our analysis is correct) will be biased as a group towards the Radical-Progressive end of the continuum. Work by McLeish (1970) and others supports this hypothesis.

The usual sociological approaches have argued from a model of the structure of the school to a model of socialization. The process of socialization has been secondary and been distorted by its function of fitting individuals into existing structures. We have reversed the normal process and we have arrived at a 'grounded theory' understanding of socialization and are using this to modify our view of the school. The school now appears as an arena in which teachers strive for two goals. The first is the most obvious and emphasized in all previous work, acceptance into and promotion within the existing structure of the school. The energies of sociologists and psychologists have produced an exceedingly rich literature on the numerous ways of studying this process. The second goal is to make the school resemble more closely the sort of place in which the teacher would like to teach. This is normally a secondary goal and in traditional, highly constrained and stable institutions it is of minor importance. However, in the present situation where new schools are being created this second goal can become of considerable importance, and in some situations of conflict it can become more important than the first. That is, teachers will take a stance that they know will damage their careers, in order to uphold a principle about how the school should run. This sort of incident is becoming more common as the variety of schools, and the difference in view as to what schools should try to achieve, grows. There is now considerable choice for the new teacher, and this in itself produces an atmosphere in which the teacher's confidence grows.

School can be seen as the arena in which opposing definitions of the school compete. The resulting structure is a result of this process as well as the many other constraining forces well documented in the literature.

The case study

The case study is introduced at this point in order to describe some of the career pressures that effect the teacher as he moves beyond the first year of his career. Very little research has been carried out on the later stages of careers and the available data is sketchy and restricted in scope. By presenting a case study with which the author is familiar it is hoped to present a more coherent picture than could be obtained by extracting scraps of information from a wide range of research styles.

The case study is presented so that career pressures are described sequentially; as they appear to have a maximum effect on the world view of the teacher. It must be remembered that the material was not collected with the aid of the theoretical framework developed in the preceding chapters; a re-interpretation will be attempted but a complete re-analysis is not possible without further fieldwork.

By the early 1960s Hightown Grammar was by conventional criteria a successful local grammar school. It had a good academic record, with one or two star pupils gaining entrance to Oxford or Cambridge each year; it had an active sporting and school society programme with its pupils gaining successes at the local and county, and more rarely national, level; it had a well-established house system and an active parents' association. It was able to attract staff of good quality, particularly from the local provincial university. The only serious problem in this respect was the difficulty in attracting well qualified science staff. Twenty-eight of the thirty-nine staff were graduates and fifteen of these came from the local university.

Young teachers joining the school found themselves allocated a position within two organizational systems, the academic department structure and the pastoral or house system. Within the rhetoric of the school and house assemblies and the occasional staff meeting, the house organization loomed large. On the other hand, the subject departments formed the basis for the day to day organization of the school, and most of the school's resources were channelled through the departments.

The two structures are summarized in the following diagram:

Table 6.5 *Academic Organization*

Headmaster
|
Deputy Headmaster
(or senior master)
|
Heads of Departments
(English, History, Geography, Economics,
French, Latin, Chemistry, Mathematics,
Physics, Biology, Art, Woodwork, Physical
Education, Music)
|
Subject Masters (some with responsibility allowances)

House Organization

Headmaster
|
Deputy Headmaster
|
Heads of House (4)
|
House group masters (24)

The channelling of resources through the two systems included the proportion of the per capita allowance for textbooks, special subject equipment and teaching aids, but also included the payment of special responsibility allowances to the masters themselves. The allocation of these responsibility allowances is summarized in the diagram which follows:

143

Table 6.6 *Cash allowances per annum* (*1963*)

	£450	£355	£260	£165	£100
Heads of depts.	English Maths.	History Geography French Chemistry	Biology Physics	Art Music Handi- crafts Latin	Physical Ed. Economics
Deputy heads				English History French Maths.	Geography
Other responsibility allowances					3rd English 2nd Chemistry 2nd Physics 2nd Biology 2nd P.E.

Heads of Houses. Allowances p.a. showing breakdown between academic and house responsibilities allowance.

£260: 1. Head of Latin (£165)   +   Head of House (£95)
       2. Head of Handicrafts (£165)   +   Head of House (£95)
£230: 3. Deputy Head of History (£165) +   Head of House (£65)
       4. Deputy Head of English (£165) +   Head of House (£65)

Thus the head of house job actually attracted a smaller responsibility allowance than the lowest academic responsibility allowance (£100).

It was very unlikely that the beginning teacher would be given a responsibility allowance in his first year of teaching, but the structure of payments and their significance for his career was not lost on members of staff.

The new teacher would also notice that the heads of departments controlled an important set of resources. The money allocated for books and teaching aids was usually spent by the head of department in consultation with other staff. In practice, only his deputy had much influence on this process. One junior teacher who was unable to influence the head of department and get a set of books he required saw this as a last straw; as a signal for him to look elsewhere for a job. As he saw it, the decision affected his everyday teaching. Without the books he required his life was made more difficult and his teaching less effective.

The most important area of control at Hightown was, however, the allocation of teaching. This was not directly in the hands of heads of departments, but they made the initial recommendations to the deputy head and the master who actually drew up the timetable. It was clear that in reallocating duties where the initial recommendation could not be met they bore in mind the two principles of organization on which the school was based – the subject of specialization and the seniority/status of the individual. Any violation of these principles brought irate and angry teachers to the deputy head's study. The extent to which types of teaching were allocated on the basis of seniority/status is demonstrated in the following table. The categories of teaching are arranged roughly in order of desirability and prestige.

Table 6.7 *Analysis of timetable for the eight academic departments with three or more members of staff, 1962–63*

	Heads of department (8)	Deputy heads (8)	Others in department (12)
	%	%	%
Non-teaching period	18·3	15·4	15·4
Sixth forms	49·4	23·7	7·4
Express streams	11·7	9·4	4·6
Fifth forms (not C streams)	6·7	14·3	9·0
Middle school third and fourth (not E or C)	8·5	14·3	15·4
First and second year (not E or C)	5·4	12·5	21·4
Bottom stream (C)	—	6·7	19·1
Games	—	3·7	7·7
Total	100·0	100·0	100·0

Note: numbers represent the average percentage of teaching periods in each type of teaching.

In fact 65 per cent of first and second year teaching and 85 per cent of bottom stream teaching was done by masters who were neither heads nor deputy heads of departments. In practice this meant that most new teachers were allocated some of both. In theory, first and second years were allocated to new teachers also because they were regarded as relatively easy to discipline. This was not always true of the more difficult second year classes and did not explain why young teachers were often allocated some very difficult classes.

This can only be explained by the working of the seniority principle.

I first noticed the seniority principle in action when, early in the research, I started classroom observations at the school. The senior master always took great care to introduce me to senior members of staff well before I visited their classrooms. I was expected to explain the research to them and confirm with them that it would be all right for me to sit in on the lesson. With junior staff the elaborate preparation was often set aside and on several occasions the senior master introduced me during the start of the lesson. It was clear that 'seniority' was frequently confirmed and reinforced by 'status' within the departmental structure. Heads of departments tended to be older than deputy heads and deputy heads older than others in the department. In two cases where the 'seniority' principle was violated by the appointment of junior more highly qualified men to deputy head of department a tense and uncertain situation developed. Both appointments gave rise to incidents that owed a great deal of their intensity to the older man's violated status aspirations.

The seniority principle was also a factor in the informal relationships within the staff. Groups within the staffroom were analysed and revealed that after subject discipline, seniority was the most important factor associated with the composition of groups.

The 'seniority principle' rested on the general understanding that as a person gained seniority within the school he took on a number of responsibilities and he was accepted as a person with an opinion that mattered and needed consulting. The accumulation of minor offices and responsibilities inevitably entailed extra work and in conversation teachers often described them as rather tiresome chores. On the other hand it was noticeable that once a teacher had become for example the second XI coach or master responsible for issuing stationery they were loath to give up the jobs unless replaced with perhaps the first XI or a more important administrative responsibility. The responsibilities were arranged in a hierarchy in which it was understood that running the school magazine was more prestigious than running the school savings bank and running the senior library more important than the junior library.

A new member of staff could expect to be approached to take up a minor responsibility in his first or second year at the school. It was noticeable that after a tentative and hesitant beginning masters became active in acquiring and expanding their responsibilities until in their 30s or 40s they had often acquired a portfolio of jobs and minor offices. Earlier in this chapter I reported a remark by a probationary teacher who felt the onset of these career pressures. He likened the profession to a 'rat-race for promotion' but felt free from the pressure while he remained unmarried. Within the fairly stable structure of a grammar school these competitive pressures were keenly felt but they were restricted to the areas of activity outside the curriculum. In schools where the curriculum is also being reorganized (as in the case of the probationer above) it provides new opportunities for the creative and experimentally minded teacher but also new uncertainties and tensions for others. The teaching profession will be confronted increasingly with these inter-peer group competitive pressures as areas of curriculum are questioned and rethought. It will need to develop new styles of collaboration if it is to carry the reassessment through successfully.

Three fairly typical examples of the 'portfolios' of masters in mid career illustrate the scope of their area of activity at Hightown Grammar.

1 *Classics master – head of house:* first XI cricket and football, cricket kit (responsible master). Visits to Italy. Responsible for report books. Represented school on local authority committees and area sports committee.
2 *Deputy head of English – head of house:* first XI cricket, editor of school magazine, football and cricket tours at home and abroad. Certified referee. School debates and interhouse debating competitions. Organized theatre visits.
3 *Science master – careers master:* very active – conferences and local contacts. Duke of Edinburgh Award Scheme (responsible master). Senior Scouts, camps, sports teams – had run first XI football.

The scope and direction of these portfolios were partly dictated by the skills and status of the individual teachers, so that the classics master ran trips to Italy and the deputy head of English edited the school magazine. It was clear that at times a competitive atmosphere developed for example, who would run the first XI and who would organize the main summer visit. At these times it was apparent that a great deal more was at stake than who would put in the extra hours of work necessary to organize the activity. In exploring this area of professional development it became clear that a number of motives were at work. There was the desire to develop a personal reputation, a presence within the school; personal space within the peer group. There was the need to develop identifiable activities that could become claims to a promotion inside the school or to another institution. Both these motives are illustrated in the following paragraphs.

A teacher's contribution to these extra curricula activities was more likely to involve recognition by headmaster, pupils and staff than his everyday classroom teaching. For example, a young master who started a judo club gained considerably in stature as a result. The club meetings were announced in morning prayers and came to the notice of the headmaster, the club flourished and attracted 6th formers who the master would not otherwise have taught. From being a person who taught French mainly to first and second years he became known throughout the school as an enthusiastic and energetic master. The activity enabled him to become a public figure. In a similar way even minor administrative duties enabled the master to have a special relationship with the headmaster or deputy head to whom he reports and acts as a central person in the distribution of a resource, for example, stationery or games equipment.

It was apparent at Hightown that these competitive pressures engaged young teachers very quickly. However, it was not until the problems of classroom control and the routine of the classroom were mastered that they emerged with greater significance. At this point in his career the young master would be eligible for a deputy head of department or later on, head of department. Even for the post of headmaster it was necessary to be able to show a broad range of activities, engaged in at the appropriate time and continued up to the present. In Hightown during the 1960s it involved active participation in organizations such as the church, scouting, local choirs, local government, local societies (e.g. history, drama) the Workers Educational Association, the Y.M.C.A. and other youth clubs; attending a wide variety of courses; having interests of a liberal and cultural nature.

The importance of these activities is emphasized in teaching where the classroom remains a relatively private place. The shape of the teacher's career therefore owes a great deal to them. The combination of pressures gave rise to a recognizable structure within the staff at Hightown Grammar.

One described the situation in a particularly graphic manner. 'This school is like a sandwich with a soft top, a soft bottom and a hard core or filling. On the top, you've got the Head and Mr Price wanting to be loved, Mr Tonkins – he's all talk – and Mr Wright, a very nice man but too soft. [All the teachers mentioned here were in their fifties or sixties.] You can't carry on like a benevolent, pipe-smoking Mr Chips. He's much too soft, his chemistry results are terrible. You've got to be prepared to drive them like Mr Wood, thumping them through History. Wright has let many a boy down in this way. The hard filling contains people like Mr Wood, Mr Lawless, Mr Werk, Mr Stevens and myself [all, including himself, were in their thirties] and the soft bottom is made up of people like Mr Cook, Mr Harris and Mr Robin, where all hell breaks loose in the classroom.' [These three teachers were all in their first or second year of teaching.]

It is clear that as well as portraying an aspect of the staff structure at Hightown Grammar, this description can be seen to coincide roughly with the stages in a teacher's career. A new master quickly becomes part of the 'soft bottom'. As he masters the techniques of teaching and his classroom control improves, he can begin to think in terms of taking on extra responsibilities. Eventually he is experienced enough to contemplate promotion and it is at this stage that he moves into the 'hard core' and becomes a prominent, forceful member of the staff. During this stage some are promoted out of grammar schools (into colleges of education or further education). The characteristics of the 'soft top' are developed most markedly in the last few years of teaching, when promotion is no longer a possibility and the teacher's energies may be sapped through illness.

The picture that emerges, of a stable structure organized around notions of seniority and status within academic departments, needs to be modified by looking again at some of the internal conflicts and by examining some of the later changes that affected the school. These were of four types – pastoral care reform, curriculum modification and change, internal reorganization, and the internal effects of comprehensive reorganization of the school.

The house system was developed at Hightown in 1956 by the then headmaster to replace the form teacher system and broaden the basis for social and community activity. It was developed in the face of tough opposition from the older members of staff who regarded themselves (not the relatively new Headmaster) as the true inheritors of the tradition of the school. The house system grew to include the following activities.

In the first year, the four house groups coincided with the academic forms. In the second year, the house groups remained, but their academic functions were removed. They now formed the basis for registration, for the distribution of free milk at morning break, and for dinners at mid-day. In addition, one morning assembly a week was given over to house prayers, conducted by the housemaster, and various games, scholastic competitions (debates, declamations) and charity activities were organized on a house basis. Finally, rewards and punishments (house points and detentions) were organized on a house basis, as were meetings with parents and the whole area of home/school relations.

The point of including this description is to show that even during this 'stable' period the school did not present a uniform 'socializing' front to new members. Teachers were able to choose between putting their energies into activities traditionally within the subject department structure or the new house system. Starting from this new option a few members of staff were able to build completely new careers which led in one case to a head of house in a new comprehensive school and in another to the creation of a new post within the school. The change created an area of uncertainty and conflict which was recorded by me in the following passage.

It will be seen that the housemasters' duties and responsibilities pervaded most aspects of school life. They were responsible for the boys in their house in a way heads of department were not. This wide range of responsibility and heavy work load, with the low rate of pay for the job, inevitably caused a certain amount of disillusionment among them. One remarked that what he received for the job did not pay his fares to school. He viewed it as 'hard work with little reward, responsibility with no power'. It was certainly true that housemasters found it difficult to get much 'co-operation' from the older members of staff who were their seniors in the departmental system. These staff, who pre-dated the house system at the school, were the ones most opposed to it and they did least to make it work. They tended to regard their responsibilities as beginning and ending with the registration of their pupils and were described to me by one head of house as 'nine-to-fourers'.

The headmaster always supported heads of houses in their attempts to awaken enthusiasm and organize the perennial house activities. But his support was of a generalized nature and normally consisted of remarks to the whole staff about the importance of the house system and how he felt sure they would 'give wholehearted support as they always had done in the past'. There was never any question of outspoken criticism of the system on such public occasions, but there was much muted criticism in discussion afterwards. Sometimes a large amount of the responsibility for getting the particular activity 'off the ground' fell back on to the housemaster. After one such meeting, a head of house remarked that I would hear a good deal about the educational and social advantages of the house system while at the school, but that I should not overlook the fact that it removed a lot of work from the headmaster's shoulders.

However, in 1963 I missed the point that *one* of the reasons the heads of house put so much energy into their poorly paid and responsible jobs was that it enabled them to get away from the restrictions of the traditional structure and build a new career. They worked hard but they obviously enjoyed their responsibilities and opportunities. Other changes affected the socializing influence of the school in the same way. The introduction of economics into the sixth form involved the appointment of a new, relatively young head of department who was also outside the old departmental structure. Other subjects have subsequently been introduced. The change from a rigidly streamed to the streamed/set structure brought the possibility of developing new classroom and pedagogic strategies. Finally, the two-stage reorganization of the school, first by merging it with a technical high school and then transforming it in to a sixth form college with a comprehensive school, with an age range of eleven to sixteen, on the same site, brought new opportunities and new problems.

The changes that have affected Hightown Grammar over the last ten years are not adequately summarized in this brief account. However, they do serve to illustrate the way in which every major aspect of the school was subject to change in a school that had seen only one major organizational change in the previous twenty years – the setting up of the house system. In analyzing the expected career pattern of young school masters joining the school in the 1960s I used the traditional method of reconstruction, working out from present and past examples, the major stages through which the career of the school teacher would pass. While this enabled me to establish a broad structure, it underestimated the extent to which the careers being started at that time were and would be different from those started ten and twenty years previously. Hightown Grammar did not conform to the stable community described by Radcliffe Brown in Chapter 1. In a period of rapid change it is often more important to concentrate on the new development and its possible spread and application than the established patterns.

Conclusion

This chapter concludes our discussion on teacher socialization. In part it has been necessarily theoretically biased because many of the studies needed to enlarge our knowledge of teacher socialization have yet to be undertaken. Most of the stages of the teacher's career after the probationary year remain unstudied and there is surely a pressing need for this omission to be remedied. Unfortunately the fact that the studies would be difficult long term research, unsuitable for both thesis students, and agencies funding short term research, means that they are likely to be rare, even in the future. However socialization can be appropriately studied in the context of shorter term institutional studies and studies of innovations if the appropriate theoretical stance is adopted. It has been a major purpose of this book to provide a suitable theoretical stance and an appropriate conceptual framework for this type of study. I have attempted to readjust the existing priority of structure over process and advocate a study of institutions through the study of socialization. Institutions can fruitfully be conceived of as areas in which social reality is constructed (Berger and Luckmann 1966) through the interplay of individual actions with changing roles and purposes.

The focus on social strategies is the key to this new approach. It is a unit of behaviour meaningful to the actor. It can be documented and can be used to establish individual purpose. Modifications of social strategies are the observed data from which the socialization process can be described and recorded. However, it is from the presenting of these descriptions to actors in the field, in this case teachers (Lacey 1976), that an appreciation of purpose and greater analytical depth can be achieved. The collaboration of teachers and researchers can result in benefit to both. The teacher can obtain an analytical appraisal of the school and his or her part within it, which can lead to more effective action in the pursuit of purpose and a professional stance with respect to pedagogy. The researcher can obtain deeper insights into the connections between the micro system (the school) studied, its social context and the individual. The sociologist has always been at his or her least penetrating in attempting to trace the mechanisms which link the individual to the micro system and the macro system to the broader society. This is most marked in recent developments in the sociology of knowledge (Young, 1971) but is a feature of most courses in sociology – methodology and theory seem all too frequently unrelated. The opportunity to bridge this gap is an opportunity which should not be ignored.

In the past it appeared self-evident that teachers needed to know about the development and the socialization of the child. Child development and the primary socialization of the child have therefore become important parts of most postgraduate and initial certificate courses. The socialization of the teacher, however, rarely features in these courses. One of the implications of the argument developed in this book is that student-teachers should be helped to become aware of the social forces structuring their perspective, but also of the inexact and partial knowledge that we have of these 'social forces'. It is within the professional role of the teacher that he or she will be able to test and experiment with them in a truly unique and creative manner.

References and
name index

Auld, Robin Q. C. (1976) *William Tyndale Junior and Infants Schools – Public Enquiry*. London: Inner London Education Authority. *27*

Barker-Lunn, J. C. (1970) *Streaming in the Primary School*. Slough: National Foundation Education Research. *37*

Becker, H. S. (1953) The teacher in the authority system of the public school. *Journal of Educational Sociology* 25: 3. *35*

Becker, H. S. (1971) *Sociological Work: Method and Substance*. London: Allen Lane. In particular 'Personal Change in Adult Life'. *72*

Becker, H. S., Geer, B. and Hughes, E. (1961) *Boys in White*. Chicago: University of Chicago Press. *9, 61, 66, 67, 69.*

Bennett, N. (1976) *Teaching Styles and Pupil Progress*. London: Open Books. *37*

Berg, L. (1968) *Risinghill – The Death of a Comprehensive School*. Harmondsworth: Penguin. *27*

Berger, P. L. and Luckmann, T. (1966) *The Social Construction of Reality*. Harmondsworth: Penguin. *20, 152*

Blumer, H. (1966) Sociological implications of the thoughts of George Herbert Mead. *American Journal of Sociology* 71. *72*

Boyson, R. (1975) The developing case for the Education Voucher. In *Black Paper 1975*, C. B. Cox and R. Boyson (eds). *22*

Butcher, H. J. (1965) The attitude of student teachers to education. *British Journal of Social and Clinical Psychology* IV. *48, 111*

Cain, B. and Schroeder, C. (1970) *The Teacher and Research.* Slough: NFER.

Chanan, G. and Delamont, S. (eds) (1975) *Frontiers of Classroom Research.* Slough: NFER. *39*

Clark, R. P. and Nisbett, J. D. (1963) *The First Two Years of Teaching.* Aberdeen: Department of Education. *46*

Cohen, A. (1955) *Delinquent Boys – The Culture of Gangs.* Glencoe, Illinois: Free Press. *61*

Cohen, L. (1969) Functional dependence, exchange and power of influence. *International Journal of Educational Science* 3. *48*

Collier, K. G. (1973) A Principal's View of College Administration. In D. E. Lomax (ed.). New York: Wiley. *52*

Cope, E. (1971) *School Experience in Teacher Education.* Bristol: University Publication. *48*

Cornwell, J. *et al.* (1965) *The Probationary Year.* Birmingham: University Institute of Education. *46*

Delamont, S. (1976) *Interaction in the Classroom.* London: Methuen. *39*

Durkheim, E. (1938) *The Rules of Sociological Method.* New York: Free Press. *19*

Edgar, D. and Warren, R. (1969) Power and Autonomy in Teacher Socialization. *Sociology of Education* XLII. *47*

Elliott, J. (1976) Evaluation. In *Progress in Learning Science.* Wynne Harlen Information Paper No. 6. London: Schools Council. *43*

Elliott, J. and MacDonald, B. (eds) (1975) People in Classrooms. *Occupational Paper No. 2.* London: Centre for Applied Research in Education. *44*

Etzioni, A. (1969) *The Semi Professions and their Organization.* New York: Free Press. *31*

Finlayson, D. S. and Cohen, L. (1967) The teacher's role: a comparative study of the conception of college of education students and headmasters. *British Journal of Educational Psychology* XXXVII. *39*

Floud, J. (1962) Teaching in the affluent society. *British Journal of Sociology* XIII. *39*

Floud, J. and Scott, W. (1961) Recruitment to Teaching in England and Wales. In A. H. Halsey, J. Floud and C. A. Anderson (eds). New York: Free Press. *35*

155

Frankenberg, R. (1970) The Sociologically Minded Person and the Self Understanding Society. Inaugural Lecture. University of Keele.

Glaser, B. and Strauss, A. (1968) *The Discovery of Grounded Theory*. London: Weidenfeld and Nicolson. *56*

Gluckman, M. (ed.) (1964) *The Limits of Naivety*. Edinburgh and London: Oliver and Boyd. *10*

Gouldner, A. W. (1971) *The Coming Crisis of Western Sociology*. London: Heinemann.

Grace, G. R. (1972) *Role Conflict and the Teacher*. London: Routledge and Kegan Paul. *39*

Hamilton, D. (1975) Handling innovation in the classroom: two Scottish examples. In W. A. Reid and D. F. Walker (eds). London: Routledge and Kegan Paul. *39*

Hannam, C. *et al.* (1976) *The First Year of Teaching*. Harmondsworth: Penguin. *45*

Hansen, D. A. and Gerstl, J. E. (1967) *On Education: Sociological Perspectives*. New York: Wiley. *25*

HMSO (1972) *Teacher Education and Training*. James Report. *50*

HMSO (1973) *Statistics of Education*. Teachers Volume. *32, 33, 36*

HMSO (1972) *A Framework for Expansion*. White Paper. *50*

Hilsun, S. and Cain, B. (1971) *The Teacher's Day*. Slough: NFER. *40*

Hoyle, E. (1969) *The Role of the Teacher*. London: Routledge and Kegan Paul. *39*

Hughes, E. C., Becker H. S. and Geer B. (1958) 'Student Culture and Academic Effort'. *Harvard Educational Review* Vol. 28. *70*

Illich, I. D. (1971) *Deschooling Society*. London: Calder and Boyars. *22*

Jackson, B. and Marsden, D. (1962) *Education and the Working Class*. London: Routledge and Kegan Paul. *70*

Jackson, J. A. (1970) *Professions and Professionalisation*. Cambridge: University Press. *31*

Johnson, T. (1972) *Professions and Power*. London: Macmillan. *31*

Kelly, S. G. (1970) *Teaching in the City*. Dublin: Gill and Macmillan. *39, 42*

Kob, J. (1961) Definitions of the teacher's role. In A. H. Halsey *et al.* (eds). New York: Free Press. *39*

Lacey, C. (1970) *Hightown Grammar*. Manchester: University Press. *11, 67, 142–52*

Lacey, C. (1976) Problems of Sociological Fieldwork. In M. Shipman. London: Routledge and Kegan Paul. *153*

Lacey, C., Horton, M. and Hoad, P. (1973) Teacher Socialization: the Post-graduate Year. In Tutorial Schools Research Project Report. *53–4, 58, 60, 62, 63, 78–87, 92–5, 101–25, 139, 140*

Leggatt, T. W. (1970) Teaching as a Profession. In J. A. Jackson. Cambridge: University Press. *31*

MacDonald, B. (1976) Evaluation and the control of education. In D. Tawney (ed.). London: Schools Council.

McEvans, I. (1976) The Animals came in Ones and Twos. *Radio Times*. London: B.B.C. Publication. *98*

McLeish, J. (1970) *Students' Attitudes and College Environments*. Cambridge: Institute of Education. *48, 64, 141*

Mead, G. H. (1934) *Mind, Self and Society*. Chicago: University Press. *66*

Merton, R. K. *et al.* (1957) *The Student Physician*. Cambridge, Mass.: Harvard University Press. *13, 14, 117*

Miller, C. and Parlett, M. (1974) *Up to the Mark*. London: Society for Research into Higher Education. *90–1*

Musgrove, F. and Taylor, P. H. (1969) *Society and the Teacher's Role*. London: Routledge and Kegan Paul. *39, 41*

Neill, A. S. (1962) *Summerhill: a radical approach to child-rearing*. London: Gollancz. *22*

Norwood, Sir C. (1943) *Curriculum and Examinations in Secondary Schools*. London: Board of Education. *22*

Oliver, R. A. C. and Butcher, H. J. (1965) Teachers' attitudes to Education – the structure of educational attitudes. *British Journal of Social and Clinical Psychology* I. *48, 59*

Oliver, R. A. C. and Butcher, H. J. (1968) Teachers' attitudes to Education. *British Journal of Educational Psychology* XXXVIII. *48, 59*

Parsons, T. (1951) *The Social System*. London: Routledge and Kegan Paul. *18, 21*

Radcliffe Brown, A. R. (1952) *Structure and Function in Primitive Society*. London: Cohen and West. *19*

Rex, J. (1961) *Key Problems of Sociological Theory*. London: Routledge and Kegan Paul. *20*

Roberts, B. (1964) Teachers' Colleges and Professional Attitudes. Ph.D. thesis: Chicago University. *51*

Rudd, W. E. A. and Wiseman, S. (1962) Sources of dissatisfaction among a group of teachers. *British Journal of Educational Psychology* XXXII. *45*

Ruddock, J. (1976) *Dissemination of Innovation: the Humanities Curriculum Project*. London: Evans/Methuen. *44*

Sharp, R. and Green, A. (1975) *Education and Social Control: a study in progressive primary education*. London: Routledge and Kegan Paul.

Snyder, B. (1971) *The Hidden Curriculum*. New York: Knopf. *92*

Stubbs, M. and Delamont, S. (eds) (1976) *Exploration in Classroom Observation*. New York: Wiley. *39*

Taylor, J. K. and Dale, I. R. (1971) A Survey of Teachers in their First Year of Service. Bristol: University Publication. *46, 47*

Taylor, W. (1969) *Society and the Education of Teachers*. London: Faber and Faber. *49*

Tropp, A. (1957) *The School Teachers*. London: Heinemann.

Walker, R. (1972) The sociology of education and life in school classrooms. *International Review of Education* 18. *39*

Walker, R. and Adelman, C. (1975) *A Guide to Classroom Observation*. London: Methuen. *39, 44*

Waller, W. (1932) *The Sociology of Teaching*. New York: Wiley. *40, 49*

Ward, L. F. (1924) *Dynamic Sociology*. New York: Appleton Century Crafts. *23*

Westwood, L. J. (1967) The Role of the Teacher. *Educational Research* IX, 2. *39*

Westwood, L. J. (1969) The Role of the Teacher. *Educational Research* X, 1. *39*

Wilson, B. (1962) The Teacher's Role: a sociological analysis. *British Journal of Sociology*. *39, 41*

Winchester, S. (1971) Another Victim in the Ardoyne. London: *The Guardian*, 30 October. *15–17*

Wiseman, S. and Start, K. B. (1965) A follow-up of teachers five years after completing their training. *British Journal of Educational Psychology* XXXV. *45*

Wrong, D. (1961) The oversocialized conception of man in modern sociology. *American Sociological Review* 26. *10, 66*

Young, M. F. D. (1971) *Knowledge and Control*. London: Collier-Macmillan/Open University. *153*

Subject index